W9-DAF-079

Twayne's United States Authors Series

EDITOR OF THIS VOLUME

David J. Nordloh

Indiana University

Will N. Harben

TUSAS 330

Will N. Harben

WILL N. HARBEN

By JAMES K. MURPHY
West Georgia College

TWAYNE PUBLISHERS
A DIVISION OF G. K. HALL & CO., BOSTON

Copyright © 1979 G. K. Hall & Co.

Published in 1979 by Twayne Publishers,
A Division of G. K. Hall & Co.
All Rights Reserved

Printed on permanent/durable acid-free paper and bound in the
United States of America

First Printing

Library of Congress Cataloging in Publication Data

Murphy, James K
Will N. Harben.

(Twayne's United States authors series ; TUSAS 330)
Bibliography: p. 156–61
Includes index.
1.   Harben, William Nathaniel, 1858–1919
—Criticism and interpretation.
PS1788.H3Z78   813'.4   78-27131
ISBN 0-8057-7245-6

In memory of my mother

Contents

About the Author

James K. Murphy is an associate professor of English at West Georgia College, Carrollton, Georgia (about one hundred miles south of Will N. Harben's native Dalton), where he has taught since 1963. A graduate of the University of Chattanooga, he received his M.A. in English from the University of Kentucky and his Ph.D. in English from George Peabody College for Teachers. A West Virginian by birth, his other teaching experiences include two years of high school teaching in Tennessee and a year of teaching grammar during his military service.

He has published several articles on Harben for national periodicals, and has co-authored two literature workbooks for high school students. He is a member of various professional organizations, including the National Council of Teachers of English, the Conference on College Composition and Communication, and the South Atlantic Modern Language Association.

Preface

Writing at the turn of the twentieth century, Will N. Harben was a sincere and accurate interpreter of rural life in North Georgia whose thirty novels and numerous short stories were in his time recognized as the best of their kind. Yet today he is largely unknown and unread. Living in a time when American literary tastes were divided between Realism and Romanticism, Harben managed to combine the two movements. He succumbed to the sentimental preferences of the public by writing many inflated, romantic tales, thereby becoming a best-selling author of his day. But he exhibited an undeniably strong realism in his portrayals of the mountaineers of his native Georgia region, an area he knew inside and out. Harben's stories and novels of this isolated country were combinations of the romance and quaintness of local color stories and the objectivity and forcefulness of serious, realistic works.

This study is an attempt to reevaluate the large body of Harben's works, analyzing them individually and collectively. Since these works are unfamiliar to most readers, basic summaries of their contents are given along with short discussions of the major themes. Harben took his hill folk more seriously than did other contemporary writers, who saw them as nostalgic inhabitants of a happy existence. Their defiance of narrow social or religious concepts of the day set Harben's characters apart, isolated from many of their peers. To Harben, they represented a group who would, in a generation or two, become the modern Southern middle class. These backwoods men and women included blacks as well as whites, and Harben's attitude toward the black man is interesting: while perceiving the inequities in their treatment by many Southerners, he was curiously sentimental in his depiction of most of his black characters. Such thematic characteristics have been applied to those works of Harben's where they are appropriate.

A brief and by no means definitive biography is offered; since

Harben left no personal papers, biographical research is an especially difficult task, and most of the information has been obtained, by necessity, in a piecemeal fashion. The first chapter describes the interests and influences of Harben's first thirty years, to the time he began writing professionally; additional biographical material is interspersed throughout remaining chapters. Chapters two through five are examinations of his works in chronological order, including one chapter devoted solely to his short stories. The last chapter is a general assessment of his works as a whole.

No attempt is made to promote Harben to major literary stature, since his excessive sentimentality in some dialogue, plots, and characters tends to mar his otherwise effective writing. But his honest and serious depictions of North Georgia mountaineers and their customs have such merit that he deserves more recognition than he presently receives.

JAMES K. MURPHY

West Georgia College

Acknowledgments

I am indebted to Dr. Warren I. Titus, George Peabody College for Teachers, for his encouragement and advice during the initial stages of the study; to Dr. James W. Mathews, West Georgia College, for introducing me to Harben; and to Dr. David J. Nordloh, Indiana University, for his perceptive and valuable editing.

I have come away from the project with a renewed appreciation of the helpfulness and cooperation of libraries everywhere, especially the West Georgia College Library; the Dalton Regional Library; the New York Public Library, which granted me permission to quote from unpublished material in the Century Collection and the Anthony Collection; the Robert W. Woodruff Library, Emory University, for allowing me to quote from the Joel Chandler Harris Collection and the Frank L. Stanton Papers; and the Duke University Library, which gave me permission to quote from the William Garrott Brown Papers.

The personnel at Harper & Row kindly made available to me their resources, and granted me permission to quote from the Harben books published by Harper and Brothers. Acknowledgment is made to the editors of the *Mississippi Quarterly, Southern Folklore Quarterly,* and *Georgia Life* for their permission to reprint material from my articles in their periodicals.

The citizens of Dalton, Georgia, who are rightly proud of their native writer, were more than generous with their time, information, and interest, especially Mrs. Aileen F. Alley, Harben's cousin, who lives in his ancestral home. Harben's immediate family were most helpful and cooperative in supplying me with invaluable information and material. My special thanks go to Harben's charming daughter, Mrs. Elizabeth Harben Cox, for her interest and willingness to supply me with all the Harben material at her disposal; his granddaughter, Mrs. Judy Harben Alger; and his grandsons, William N. Harben and George Harben. Without their aid and cooperation, this book would have been impossible.

Chronology

1858 William Nathaniel Harben born July 5 at Dalton, Whitfield County, Georgia, son of Nathaniel Parks Harben and Myra Richardson Harben.

1878 Left school to open a general store with his brother Walter.

1884 Father died.

1885 Sold store; moved to Texas, where he opened novelty shops in Denison and Sherman.

1886 Walter Harben died; sold his Texas businesses, opened novelty store in Knoxville, Tennessee.

1887 Began translating German stories into English.

1888 Wrote and sold some short stories of his own; sold business in Knoxville, embarked on literary career; went to Europe with friend, Robert Loveman, a Dalton poet.

1889 Settled in New York; published first book, *White Marie.*

1891 *Almost Persuaded;* became an editor at *Youth's Companion* in Boston.

1892 *A Mute Confessor.*

1893 Left job at *Companion* to devote full time to writing and returned to New York; mother died; travelled in Europe and England.

1894 Settled in New York again; *The Land of the Changing Sun.*

1896 "From Clue to Climax," detective novel, published in *Lippincott's Monthly Magazine;* married Maybelle Chandler, July 2, in Dalton while on summer visit; to Europe on honeymoon; settled in New York.

1898 *The Caruthers Affair.*

1899 *The North Walk Mystery;* son William Chandler born.

1900 *Northern Georgia Sketches,* collection of ten of his best short stories.

1901 *The Woman Who Trusted; Westerfelt.*

1902 *Abner Daniel.*

1903 *The Substitute;* son Eric Marion born.

1904 *The Georgians.*
1905 *Pole Baker.*
1906 *Ann Boyd.*
1907 *Mam' Linda.*
1908 *Gilbert Neal.*
1909 *The Redemption of Kenneth Galt.*
1910 *Dixie Hart; The Fruit of Desire* by "Virginia Demarest."
1911 *Nobody's* by "Virginia Demarest"; son Eric died; *Jane Dawson.*
1912 *Paul Rundel.*
1913 *The Desired Woman;* daughter Elizabeth born.
1914 *The New Clarion.*
1915 *The Inner Law.*
1916 *Second Choice.*
1917 *The Triumph.*
1918 *The Hills of Refuge.*
1919 Died August 7, at his home in New York City; buried in Dalton, Georgia; *The Cottage of Delight,* published posthumously.
1920 *The Divine Event,* published posthumously.

CHAPTER 1

Preparatory Years: 1858-1888

WILL N. Harben once stated that his birthplace, Dalton, Georgia, was decidedly the most literary village of its size in America. "No New England town of the same population that I know anything about can be compared to it."[1] Harben was so proud of his hometown, which is nestled between two hills near the Cohutta Mountains of north Georgia in Whitfield County, that he celebrated it as "Darley" in many of his best novels and short stories. He became a realistic interpreter of rural life in the South through his sound and at times powerful renderings of Darley and its various citizens—plain townspeople, aristocratic scions, and social outcasts—and he effectively used his accumulated knowledge of this small town throughout his career.

I Boyhood: The Dreamer

Born on July 5, 1858, William Nathaniel Harben was the fourth of six children born to Myra Richardson and Nathaniel Parks Harben. His first American ancestor on his father's side, Nathaniel Harben, came to Virginia in 1625 from Newton House, Somersetshire, England. Will's paternal grandmother was Hester Boone, niece of Daniel Boone, the Kentucky pioneer. Through his mother Will claimed descent from the prominent Bowman family of Virginia and Kentucky, pioneers in the colonial and military history of these states, and from William Cosby, colonial governor of New York in 1732-1736. As a young man, Will's social aspirations awakened his interest in the Harben ancestry, and he persisted in asking his parents questions in the hope of finding a relative descended from English aristocracy. Finally, by correspondence, he made connection with the English Harben family through two lines, one by marriage into a baronage and the other through a branch of the family which had been

15

honored by Queen Victoria's knighting of Sir Henry Harben, a
nouveau-riche who had given half a million dollars to a charity
hospital shortly before the queen's Jubilee.[2] Will was soon on
terms of visiting intimacy with Sir Henry and his family, and he
dedicated one of his detective novels to them in 1898.[3]

Myra Richardson, a potential artist according to one of her
daughters, had married Nathaniel Parks Harben at the age of
sixteen. She was a sensitive, pretty woman and a kind,
understanding mother who loved her children. Her husband was
a strong, magnetic, handsome man who seemed branded for
success. A Southern planter and a prosperous speculator in gold
mining properties in North Carolina, he had also invested in
small farms near Dalton and in stores and real estate in the town.
During the gold craze in the late 1840s, he made two
unsuccessful trips to California to speculate further, spending a
year each time, but he returned the second time when his second
child, Tommie, died suddenly.[4] He never went back to California, but, like Will later, he apparently had the adventurous
Boone spirit in him that prompted him to try his fortune in the
still unsettled country of the West.

The father's complete opposition to the institution of slavery
put him in conflict with many of his fellow townspeople, and he
was frequently referred to as a "black republican," a term
especially embarrassing to Will and his brother as they were
growing up. The elder Harben had gone through many dangers
during the Civil War to stand by his convictions and to remain
loyal to the Union. The Rebel army once raided his house, and he
and his family, including Will, were forced to take refuge in the
mountains of North Carolina where Myra had been born.[5] His
only experiences in slave-owning had been in having two house
servants thrust upon him in payment for a bad debt. He kept
them only until he saw that emancipation was sure to come; they
were then given their freedom, but were allowed to stay until
they found other homes.[6] On the whole, however, the elder
Harben was a respected, powerful man in his community. Will
was therefore raised in an atmosphere of comfort and refine-
ment.

The Harben home was an old fashioned, two-storied brick
house with ten rooms and a long, white veranda, surrounded by
extensive grounds on one of the most exclusive streets in Dalton,
where Will spent his childhood, youth, and young manhood. His

older brother Tommie had died before Will was born; his oldest sisters were named Matilda Frances Harben and Georgia Monterey Harben. Frances married Captain Eldorado Ray Knight, a Federal soldier who had fought for the Union during the Civil War; "Brother Ray," a railroad official, was readily accepted by the family and became a third son to the proud parents. About the same time, Georgine, as she was called by her family, married John Miller, a former Rebel soldier, but their marriage was a trying one since John, a jeweller, was out of work so often. The two brothers-in-law, diverging politically, "managed to behave like human beings to each other."[7] Myra's favorite child, Walter LaFayette Harben, was only two years younger than Will, and while Will had a magnetic smile and a straightforward manner which made him a favorite with little effort on his part, Walter was more dignified and reserved. Two brothers could hardly have differed more than did Will and Walter, yet they complemented each other and were devoted companions during their youth and young manhood. Katherine, their youngest sister, was ten years younger than Will, and since Frances and Georgine were already married, the two brothers and Sister Kate were especially close. The brothers spent much of their time affectionately teasing Kate. "I was still only a girl-baby to them. . . . They had thought I was a chicken in the house when they heard me cry the first morning. That's why they all called me 'chicken' sometimes."[8]

It was a happy household, and Will was a fun loving and active boy, but independent and proud even as a child. Kate recalled a story of his childhood which expressed his protest against the right of any individual to step into the sacred precinct of another's sensitivity. As a little boy his curly hair was often praised; but, boy-like, he was as ashamed of his curls as he was of the name his family friends used for him, "Willie Harben." One of Mrs. Harben's callers was tactless enough to say, "Willie, what a pretty, curly-haired boy you are!" With no hesitancy, as if by rights of etiquette, Will replied, "And you are a freckle-faced woman!" From that point on, "Willie" became "Will" to everyone, and his curls were seldom mentioned.[9]

Will's first public appearance was on a circus day in Dalton. Dressed in an oriental garb furnished by the show people, he rode in a parade through town on an elephant, by way of which, in addition to his carrying water to the animals, he earned his admittance to the big performance under the tent.[10] Thus, in one respect at least, his childhood was typical of life in a small Southern town.

But he was more sensitive than other boys and was a habitual daydreamer. He later declared that in his dreams he always pictured himself a literary man, writing soul stirring tales of romance and mystery and having the delight of seeing them in print. When he was quite small, he would compose puzzles and riddles and send them to weekly story papers. He was in the cornfield of his father's plantation when a family servant brought him the paper containing his first published puzzle. After he became a successful writer, he stated that he had felt as lively a thrill of delight at that moment as he later did on receiving an encouraging letter or a substantial check from a magazine editor.[11]

Will was educated in the public schools of Dalton and through private tutoring, but at an early age he rebelled against the restraints of school and became an indifferent student. Though he was exceptionally bright and a close observer of details, he himself admitted that his usual position in class was at the bottom. He was more engrossed in writing romantic fiction in the manner of James Fenimore Cooper—having learned to write by studying the Leatherstocking Tales—than in learning Latin or mathematics. Apparently his gift for writing was not inherited, for the only relative who could be considered an author was an uncle, the Reverend Tyre R. Harben, his father's brother, who, before the Civil War, wrote theological treatises and denounced the novel as the work of the devil.[12] But even as a boy, Will had the gift.

When he was about twelve years old, he began to try to write stories, and once when it was his turn to read from anonymous works in magazines and newspapers—a weekly school routine— he recited the first two chapters of the first book he ever attempted to write, "Old Buckskin, the Silent Hunter of the Great West."[13] He read it with an air of unconcern, so that the teacher would not suspect its authorship. It was a blood-curdling romance, and at a climactic point, Will abruptly terminated the story with the announcement: "to be continued in our next." The story was received with marked disfavor by the teacher, who said it was evidently copied from a trashy story paper. But the tale met with enthusiasm on the playground later, and when Will

Harben announced himself the author, he became the hero of the hour among his schoolmates; he was implored to continue the story the following Friday. However, just as the bloodthirsty villain had begun a speech in broken English, the relentless teacher interrupted the performance by demanding that the manuscript be thrown into the fire.[14]

Will entertained his family as well as his school friends. It was a custom of the Harbens to gather in the sitting room after dinner. "Sometimes Georgine and John and Sister and Brother Ray would be there."[15] Will, a natural musician, though he had never had a lesson, often enlivened the family activities by playing the flute—which he had bought out of his small allowance—or the family piano. His vivid imagination and storytelling frequently relieved the boredom. At these domestic gatherings, usually he would sit for a short time absorbedly writing, snickering to himself at intervals. When bubbling over with pleasure with the result, he would read to Kate the wild flight his imagination had taken. His fantasies were always of the humorous type, much like his habit of punning. But his flights seemed to Kate "to find no solid ground of real meaning, like Noah's dove."[16] Later Kate was to be proud of her brother's success, but she became one of his severe literary critics and at times gave the impression that she thought he was prostituting himself by curbing his natural literary abilities and giving in to popular tastes. Kate once considered being a writer herself, "not like Will, but digging deep within for materials." Will's reply to her was, "Yes, and starving to death in an old maid's cold-boarding-house-attic, writing about mysteries which the world is too busy to care beans about. Kate, you are a fool." Kate grudgingly agreed; but "at any rate there seemed to be plenty of room in my Fool's Paradise for me and my dreams, too. The other Fools seemed to me to be getting crowded somewhat in their Popular Paradises."[17]

When Will was a teenager, the religious ideas of his father were a significant influence and source of embarrassment to him. The elder Harben helped a group of conservative Northern Methodists organize a new church, and the strict, orthodox rules he demanded caused the more liberal Will to completely avoid the new church. He went elsewhere.[18]

As teenagers, Will and Walter were handsome boys with the ability to make friends and to be sought after for social

gatherings. Because they would slip out together after dinner to
go to a party or to a favorite outdoor rendezvous of the town
boys, their epicurean life soon began to overshadow their school
work. They seemed innately opposed to study, considering it
drudgery. Besides, "Will was studying life—people! Books could
wait."[19] They went to picnics, dances, moonlight house parties,
drinking parties; they slept late in the mornings, much to their
father's indignation, and they played hooky repeatedly. The
family began to be troubled about Walter's passion for wine, a
fear that increased as the boys approached manhood and went
into homes where wine was served—as it emphatically was not in
the Harben household.

One night the boys had gone out without permission and
without telling where they were going. Sister Kate was
awakened around midnight by a disturbance downstairs:

Father stood at one side of the room, like an angry God, with a big,
strong switch in his hand. Mother, weeping and frightened, held on to
his arm. Father laid down the law and closed his jaws like a vise. Unless
certain revelations and promises were made at once, he was going to
whip both boys. Mother knew they were too well grown to submit. All
three were at white heat. Walter, his blue eyes aglint, his cheeks
aflame, probably with wine as well as with anger, looked searchingly
from Father to Mother. He was not afraid; he knew Mother would
never allow him to be struck. Will stood with his brown eyes brilliant,
excited, doubtful—because he shouldn't like to have to strike
Father back; Father was a powerful man. At this crisis, I entered,
screaming, to throw myself in front of Father, grasping his other arm
not held by Mother. . . . My screaming entrance saved the night. The
boys made the required promise to tell next time where they were
going.[20]

The idle life Will and Walter were living could not go on,
according to their father: they either had to make good at school
or be put to work—hard labor, anything. At the time, Mr.
Harben had a suburban farm without a tenant. He decided to
postpone other projects and take the boys to live for the summer
in the farm shack, to train them in primitive agricultural
knowledge. They took food for five days each week and came
back to Dalton for the weekends. The scheme, carried out for
one season, was not repeated. The experiment proved by process
of elimination a wise one, because the boys decided definitely
that whatever work might be necessary to make a living, that

work would not be farming.[21] A more serious consequence of the trip was an accident the elder Harben had while on the farm. Thrown from a wagon when his horse bolted, he lay unconscious for some time without the boys' knowledge. He had no reason to think he had been seriously hurt, and the mishap went almost unnoticed for several years; but damage to his brain caused by the accident ultimately led to his death.[22]

The problem of the boys' restlessness was thus not so easily solved, but Will's imagination and his sudden consciousness of his own personal magnetism furnished him, at least, with a way out: "He found that, by the clever use of his twinkling brown eyes and personal charm, he controlled an electro-magnetic weapon."[23] Though he had always been extremely popular with the girls, at eighteen he became immersed in what seemed to be his first serious love affair. The emotional situation furnished an outlet for him before the affair spent itself safely, and Will became less interested in carousing and more interested in additional dalliances with girls. He began to flirt outrageously, simply to test his charm. When no other woman was at hand, he would practice on his mother and sisters.[24]

II   *Young Adulthood: The Businessman*

The brothers, having positively rebelled against further confinement in school, in 1878, when Will was twenty and Walter eighteen, decided to leave Crawford High School for Boys to open a general store in partnership. One of their father's storerooms, empty at the time, was selected for the site. They arranged to buy a stock of goods and groceries on a credit plan, while the family waited to see if the elder Harben would come forward with additional money to help them. He decided to wait and see if the new businessmen had the grit to proceed without him. They did, and, when Harben's Emporium was a going concern, the young men's proud father paid for their stock of goods and gave them a small surplus as well. The social activities of the brothers, which had looked to their family like a waste of time, became a solid foundation for their business venture. Their friends and the families of their friends naturally began trading with them; everybody wanted to help them. The two young men were busy, and Will especially was all life and energy.[25]

Although Will and Walter were in a measure successful in their

business establishment, they were not specially fitted for
business life. They refused credit to no one and were just as
careless in paying their own bills. Will still gave himself up to his
daydreams to the extent that he would steal off and pass whole
days at a time living an adventurous life in the imaginary
surroundings that his fancy conjured up. He could not shake this
practice, nor did he wish to—but it was his secret shame
nevertheless. He was constantly afraid someone would discover
his world of refuge and hold him up to ridicule and scorn; he
dreaded being called a dawdler and idler because of what he felt
in a grown man to be a weakness. He looked around him and saw
his friends doing well, and he threw himself into his business with
enthusiasm and determination. He later laughed at these early
struggles and the desperate pride that drove him on. While he
never made a brilliant success at any of his business ventures, he
never really failed at any of them either.[26]

His literary work was still a hobby rather than a profession,
and his greatest talent then, as always, was for making friends—
of all classes, all ages, both sexes. Every human being had
something to tell him, and he used much of what he heard in his
later stories and novels. The townspeople of Dalton, the relations
from the country, the mountaineers from the nearby Cohutta
Mountains—all were his teachers, preparing him for his real
work of character painting. Harben's Emporium became a
favorite place for loafers, and the sessions around the stove
frequently were gatherings in which the wit and repartee had a
homespun flavor and wisdom. In fact, Will spent much of his time
talking with his mountain friends and writing stories about them
on wrapping paper. He would become so interested in conversation or in a checker game in the rear of the store that such leisure
became much more appealing for him than trade from any
customer. If a customer came into his store while a game was in
progress, Will and his friends would duck under a counter and
hide until the customer would leave, thinking the proprietor was
not there. To Will's thinking, business should not interfere with
pleasure.[27]

Will was an extremely popular young man in Dalton. During
his proprietorship of the store, he entered a six-hour walking
match at the city park. People came in from the country, and
everybody in town was there to cheer the sprinters on. The gate
receipts, which amounted to about fifty dollars, were to go to the

champion. When the contest closed, Will N. Harben was pronounced the winner, having walked twenty-nine and a half miles.
Once again Will was the hero of the hour. For months afterward,
when the neighboring farmers came to Dalton, they took their
children to Harben's Emporium and pointed proudly to their
champion.[28]

Will was also briefly attracted to showmanship and exploita-
tion. One summer he and a friend purchased a five-legged calf,
determined to make a fortune from this freak of nature. Leaving
the store under the supervision of Walter, they started on a tour
of the South, planning to exhibit the animal and get rich from
admission fees. They showed the calf in Birmingham, Mobile,
and New Orleans; but when they reached Texas, the calf died,
the partnership automatically dissolved, and the two young men
returned home.[29] His showmanship also was revealed in his
theatrical productions in Dalton. One such production was "Lena
Rivers"; Will was the hero, and a prominent young married lady
of the town the heroine. Kate reported that one night at home
Will sat musing happily about a recent rehearsal of the play
when suddenly he came out with a remark "which, for some
reason, has stuck in my memory, though sex-psychology was
unknown to the average person in those days, especially to young
girls: 'Gee, it would be interesting to have a real love affair with
a charming married lady!' "[30]

He probably never had such an affair, but even as a local
businessman Will loved both a good time—and "the girls." He
made a habit of running out of his store to catch little girls he
knew—particularly those whose older sisters he knew. To these
little girls, the excitement of the daily pilgrimage to town was
being held by the tall Mr. Harben while he asked questions
concerning big sister's sweethearts.[31] In fact, Will's social charm
had led him into several romances already, and he was aware of
the ease with which he could enchant any particular woman who
seemed for a time to be his complement. But inwardly he was
seeking "a vision of a human light that never was on land or sea."
He wanted perfection in a woman. Sister Kate's testy argument
was, "Can you satisfy the needs of a woman who is also
demanding perfection?"[32]

Kate decided to be a matchmaker and introduced her brother
to one of her older friends, a young lady named Floy, who was
the "perfect lady" that Will wanted, in Kate's eyes. As time went

on, gossip had it that Will and Floy were engaged. But eventually their engagement was broken, although Will later confided to Kate that he had attempted a reconciliation with Floy at a party, but that she "gave me no overwhelming welcome, did not fall into my manly arms in the presence of a roomful of gossipy people." Floy soon moved to Texas, where she married a wealthy retired dentist.[33]

In school languages had not appealed to Will, but once launched into the mercantile business he developed an interest in German, and gathered about him all those members of the Georgia community who spoke German. He had formed a close friendship with Robert Loveman, a Dalton poet his own age. The Loveman family, German Jews,[34] further inspired his interest in the language. Will often visited a Mr. Knorr, a German immigrant who ran a small shop in Dalton,[35] and their conversations led Harben to serious study; he soon mastered the language and was able to speak it fluently.

In the meantime, as a result of his accident years before, Will's father became mentally unbalanced. Will and his brother-in-law Ray Knight, who lived across the street, took the elder Harben to a private sanitarium for mental cases in Cincinnati to determine the extent of his illness. After three months it was decided that he could not get well. Brought back home, he had to be watched closely since he constantly tried to walk to the railway station to go on imagined business trips. Fortunately he had to pass his sons' store to get there, so they always managed to catch him. He died in January, 1884.[36]

For a good while Will and Walter had been yearning for more ambitious business opportunities than Dalton offered, but they stayed in the little town while their father's financial affairs were being adjusted. Finally, in 1885, they sold their store in Dalton. Merchandising as a life's work did not appeal to Walter, who moved to New York City to speculate in the stock market and to try out other business ideas. He was unsuccessful in all his attempts, and—unknown to his family at the time—was drinking more and more and also beginning to rely on morphine in the course of battling his alcoholism.[37]

Will had become obsessed with a "get-rich-quick" idea for a five-and-ten-cent store, and since the Western frontier was considered the Promised Land to many young men, he decided to become a part of the Westward Movement. His adventurous Daniel Boone spirit drew him to Texas, where he opened a novelty store in the town of Denison, near Dallas. In her romantic way, Kate always wondered whether the fact that Floy was living nearby had anything to do with this move. "After my marriage, when Will and I were both on a visit to Mother, he told me that he had been to see Floy during his stay in Texas and that they had confided to each other my part in the effort to bring them together after their estrangement. They had a good laugh at my expense."[38]

One of the Dalton papers, the *North Georgia Citizen*, later boasted that Harben's first contribution to the literary world was his Texas letters to its citizens.[39] Through the newspaper ads Harben was writing for his store, he met George Dealy, publisher of the Dallas *Morning News*, who encouraged him to write professionally.[40] But Will was still too engrossed in the merchandising business to seriously consider the idea. His novelty store was so successful in Denison that he opened a branch store in Sherman, Texas, about ten miles away. Meanwhile, because of the failure of his business hopes, Walter had sunk deeper and deeper into the world of alcohol and morphine. When Will heard of Walter's troubles, he sent for his brother to come to Sherman to take charge of the branch store there.[41]

Walter ran the store well enough, but he became increasingly depressed and morbid. After several months, Will was called by telegram from Denison to Sherman, where Walter was dying from an overdose of morphine in his boarding house. Whether his death was accidental or intentional, the family never knew because Walter died just as Will arrived in Sherman. Will accompanied his brother's body back to Dalton for the burial. He did not easily absorb the shock of his beloved brother's death and later remarked, "I admired him more than any man I have ever known in my life."[42]

Partly because of Walter's death and partly because of the return of the old restlessness, the old horror of routine, Will decided he had had enough of the wild and woolly West, so in 1886 he sold his Texas businesses and moved to Knoxville, Tennessee, where he opened still another novelty shop. In Knoxville his store proved to be quite successful, as usual, through the use of his social talents. He also became seriously

interested in a woman whose wealthy family ranked among the
social leaders of the city. In a short time Will wrote his own
family of his engagement to the girl. He asked each sister to
write a friendly letter welcoming Anne into their family, which
they did. Kate noted, "I think it was three times I performed the
same kind of sisterly service in my charming brother's long
experience in the 'Charm School' in which he was born."[43] But
the engagement was soon broken, possibly because Anne was too
independent an individual to take a subordinate role to Will.

III   Manhood: The Beginning Writer

One summer in Knoxville, Will made use of his knowledge of
German and translated a German short story, which he sent to a
weekly story paper. Accepted, its publication inspired him to
further such work. He translated a number of short stories from
the German and finally a novel, *The Lost Paradise* by Moritz Von
Reichenbach, which was published as a serial in the Atlanta-
based periodical *The Sunny South*.[44]

Harben's success with his German translations led him to think
that he should try his hand at original composition. As he had
done in Texas, he had been writing such original advertisements
for his store that they attracted considerable local attention.
Again friends advised him to adopt literature as a profession. He
began to take particular notice of the short stories which
appeared in the Atlanta *Constitution*—clear, sensational, unique
stories of fixed length. As he read them month after month, he
became convinced that he could produce something of equal
merit. During the second year he spent in Knoxville, he sent
occasional contributions to the *Constitution*. His confidence
grew when they were all accepted and published.[45]

The first story he submitted was "White Jane," the story of a
white slave. He sent it with trepidation, but it was approved by
the paper's famed columnist, Joel Chandler Harris, and its editor,
Henry W. Grady, then the literary arbiters of the South. Both
men assured the author of success; Harris complimented him
particularly on his Southern dialects. Years later in a letter to
Harris, Harben expressed his gratitude to the famous author of
the Uncle Remus stories: "When you told me . . . in the office of
the Constitution that I could succeed in story writing you did me
the greatest favor of my life, for often when about to give up and

quit I thought of your encouragement and stuck to it, till now I find myself able to earn a modest living in the most delightful profession known to workers."[46]

In fact, as the continued encouragement and criticism of Harris and Grady stimulated Harben to more strenuous efforts, he began to send his work to national publications. When he sent "White Jane" to the *Youth's Companion,* a highly respected Boston magazine, he immediately felt he had made a fool of himself. But he received a check for twenty-five dollars from the *Companion,* along with a letter from the editor inviting him to continue his contributions. The editor also sent a dozen issues of his periodical, advising the author to study them in order to have a clearer idea of the type of material the magazine published.[47] Within the next few years, story after story followed in rapid succession, meeting with ready acceptance in other national publications.

Harben found that all his daydreaming and castle building had done him a real service; it had trained his imagination as nothing else could have done, proving to have been the best preparation for his work. A local Dalton paper reported that Harben had received very complimentary references to his published short stories while in Knoxville: "His productions have a vein of originality running through the lines and sentences which is quite charming, and a competent critic has observed that Mr. Harben's sketches were the best of the kind that he had seen."[48]

In 1888, after two years in Knoxville and at the age of thirty, Harben decided that his writing ability had won him sufficient recognition to allow him to give up his business and devote his entire time to literary work. He sold his store and returned to his hometown briefly before trying his fortune as a writer. He received a modest income from real estate holdings in Dalton and from stock in the cotton factory there. He decided he would settle in New York City—but first took a trip to England and Europe with his Dalton friend, the poet Robert Loveman.

The quaint, homely, and irreverent humor of the two writers is illustrated by the habit they adopted of comparing everything they saw in Europe to buildings in Dalton. The Baptist Church in Dalton had a steeple which was the wonder of the youth of the town. So when Harben and Loveman viewed the Eiffel Tower or some other marvel of architecture, they would compare it to the height of the Baptist Church steeple. They did not know French

well enough to speak it fluently, so in order to impress the
waiters in cafes in Paris, they repeated very rapidly all the
strange geographic names they could think of, such as Chicka-
mauga, Chattahoochee, Cherokee, Okefenokee, and
Natchitoches.[49]

The trip proved to be profitable as well as pleasurable, for
during it Harben wrote his first novel. One of his chief
philosophies of writing was that the best work is done after living
in the setting of the work, absorbing the material, and then
leaving the scene and looking back on it from the distance.
"Realities in that sort of prospective [sic] seem fairly to float in
and be caressed by a haze of mystic tenderness. My first Georgia
novel was written partly in London, continued among the
students at Oxford, and finished in a bedroom of a Paris *pension,*
where I and two other American writers worked one cold winter
that we might save the expense of more than one fire."[50]

Thus Harben left his business ventures behind and committed
himself to a literary career. It would take eleven more years of
experimental writing before he would discover that his own
native soil, the North Georgia area around Dalton, was his forte.
The thirty years of his life that had been spent primarily in that
area would serve him well once he commenced writing of it.

CHAPTER 2

Experimental Years: 1889–1900

THE eleven years between 1889 and 1900 mark Harben's experimental writing period. While searching for a place in the literary world during these years, he published seven novels: one about interracial subjects, one on the discrepancy between religious profession and performance, one highly touted but inferior romance, one science-fiction story, and three detective stories in the Edgar Allan Poe–Arthur Conan Doyle vein. He also wrote many short stories, which will be discussed in a separate chapter. The consequence of this experimental period was the realization that his real talents lay in treating his own environment and his unsophisticated mountain neighbors in Georgia. But the period is also important for its showing us his versatility and his development as a writer.

I White Marie

White Marie: A Story of Georgia Plantation Life, Harben's first novel, was an expansion of his story, "White Jane." Despite its being published in Cassel and Company's "Sunshine Series" in 1889, this melancholy book became one of the most controversial of its time. Critics expressed diametrically opposed viewpoints concerning its merits. While one indicated that the book showed no literary merit and that the author had no "pen of fire,"[1] another proclaimed it to have "the fire and elan prophetic of future success."[2] A third critic, denouncing it as typical of the trash being written, considered the author a blunderer whose ignorance of the people of his section resulted in graceless and dreary pages showing no genius;[3] in contrast, still another critic commended Harben on his knowledge of his region and felt the novel worthy of preservation because of its portrayal of conflicting emotions and its strength and movement in plot.[4]

In the preface Harben states that his story is based on a tale
told him by an old exslave, Aunt Jane Richardson, a well-known
local character of Whitfield County, Georgia. He admits that
some events in the novel are eccentric—unpleasant flights of
fancy rather than actualities—but for the most part it is Aunt
Jane's true history. She had been the property of some first
cousins of Harben's mother; hence her surname was also
Richardson, a custom of slave-holding aristocracy. Kate Harben,
with Will when he first met Jane, reported that the woman "was
tanned as most workers on Southern farms are, but her skin and
light brown hair were soft and her eyes were blue."[5] She had a
black husband and a brood of dusky children and grandchildren,
had been a slave up to the Emancipation, and claimed to be of
pure white blood. Harben's imagination was fired as he became
better acquainted with Jane; he saw the potential for a powerful
story. Whether he succeeded in achieving this power is a matter
of critical debate.

Set on a plantation near Atlanta in preCivil War days, the story
relates the sad life of Marie, a white girl who has been reared
from infancy by Suzette, a Negro slave. Marie instinctively
recognizes—and the reader early suspects—her own birthright
and the racial differences which separate her from the other
slaves. Much later in the novel Harben confirms the fact that
Marie is actually the illegitimate daughter of an aristocratic
woman of the South, and that the real mother had given Marie to
Suzette, her faithful servant, in order to avoid any scandal in her
wealthy family.

At the age of fourteen Marie is sold, along with Suzette, to
Colonel Bickerstaff, an "average Southern slaveholder." At the
Bickerstaff plantation Suzette protects Marie, never allowing her
to perform the menial tasks assigned to slaves; and within four
years, Marie matures into a beautiful, warm, educated young
woman. When Harry, the handsome son of the Bickerstaffs, is
snakebitten, Marie saves his life, and the two young people fall in
love, though they will not admit the fact even to themselves.
Mrs. Bickerstaff and Harry accompany some summer guests from
Charleston back to South Carolina and stay for a visit. Johnson,
the colonel's bigoted, vindictive overseer, who is already jealous
of Marie and the preferential treatment the Bickerstaffs give
her, has witnessed one of the innocent meetings between Harry
and Marie, and tells Colonel Bickerstaff about it, maliciously
exaggerating what he has seen. The usually perceptive, fair-

minded Colonel Bickerstaff is incensed, orders Johnson to take action in any way he sees fit, and leaves to join his wife and son in Charleston. In an incredibly melodramatic scene, Johnson forces Marie to marry Jake, a black man; when Harry hears of the marriage, he rapidly becomes a debaucher and is killed in a drunken brawl. The Bickerstaffs, who never recover from their personal tragedy, scorn Marie completely and allow their plantation to go to ruin. They both eventually die of heartbreak.

Harben then allows forty years to lapse before taking up Marie's story again in the last chapter. She has become unhappily reconciled to her fate, has had children by Jake, and is now a grandmother. Suzette, on her deathbed, tells Marie the truth about her birth, already suspected by the white slave. The story becomes local gossip, and the townspeople now permit Marie to attend the white church; when she dies, she is buried in the white cemetery. The story ends tragically for all concerned.

Harben indeed had a promising situation to work with, but handled it awkwardly. *White Marie* was his first novel, and certain concessions should be made on that account. But the book would have been stronger without the gap of forty years: Harben completely overlooked the dramatic possibilities of Marie's married life before she was an old woman. Also, many of Harben's descriptive passages are overwritten. Too often he uses ornate, artificial words when simple ones would work better; he too often takes the most roundabout rather than the most direct way of making a statement: "Mrs. Bickerstaff sat down immediately on her return to her sitting-room and indited a letter to her brother-in-law in Louisiana, in which she gave diffuse expression to her surprise over and interest in the strange white-skinned slave he had been the agent in securing for them, and importuned him to make inquiries concerning the child's history." At another point in the novel, two characters are swinging from a makeshift tree swing: "The scapegrace casts an amused figure at his quaking progenitor, and with bending knee propels himself still higher."[6] The novel contains too many such passages, which tend to mar the effect Harben would have achieved had he been simpler and more direct in his diction. As one critic expressed it, "The author, rhetorically speaking, lets too many roses bloom in the fall of the year. The general public, however, is fond of roses, and it is hard to belabor them with flowers."[7]

On the other hand, there are some passages which show

Harben's promise in portraying moving, simply-stated—almost understated—emotions. Several critics also found in his expression a grace and polish not too frequently encountered in novels of the day. "If all the fiction of the hour was up to the graceful level as 'White Marie,' the critic's task would indeed be a pleasant one."[8] The agony Harry feels when he first realizes he loves Marie is an example:

He was miserable—he knew not why. He raised his gun and fired at a couple of chirping sparrows resting on the limb of a tree. One flew off, the other fell fluttering to the grass with a broken wing. He ran to it, and seeing it suffering, he shuddered and killed it with the stock of his gun, wondering how he could have been so thoughtless. Then he threw his eyes again after Marie's retreating figure, and sat down on a log and put his feverish face in his hands. He could feel Marie's light touch on his shoulders, her warm breath on his face, as he took her in his arms. He was hot, nervous, unhappy.[9]

Harben used three dialects in *White Marie*, and he succeeded admirably in two of them. The low, backwoods English of Johnson and his vulgar family is both realistic and convincing; Harben obviously knew and lived among people who spoke in this manner. His blacks always talk like stereotypical blacks, yet their speech rings true and clear and colorful. But he fails in reproducing the speech of the aristocratic whites, as they never talk like anyone human, even in their own era and condition. The dialogue he gives them is ultra-correct, artificial, and unconvincing in every respect. Unfortunately, Harben was never able to overcome this deficiency in his later works.

His characterizations are also inconsistent. To begin with, the figures are all familiar ones: the beautiful slave girl, the infatuated young master, the old planter, the cruel overseer— they are all there. The wronged heroine is a rather colorless young woman, figuratively as well as literally; though Harben deals with her sympathetically, Marie remains a mere figurehead, statuelike, with none of the fire and individuality that characterized so many of his later heroines. Harry is the typical, dashing hero of Romantic novels, and his descent at the end is incongruous with his earlier strong character. The Southern planters, Colonel and Mrs. Bickerstaff, are devoid of any real individuality. Though their dialect is realistic, Johnson and his family, representing the poor white trash of the South, are so unbelievably crude and brutal that they become caricatures of villains, utterly implausible as persons. Only in his quaint sketches of black characters and manners does Harben reveal his abilities to depict authentic people. His descriptions of the gossip, gabble, and rivalries of the slaves are skillful. In their activities there is an entertaining vein of quiet humor which relieves the general somber tone of the narrative. The boastful self-importance of Pomp, the butler of the plantation, and the energetic culinary pride of Poll, the cook, are especially good depictions.

Yet the ambiguity of Harben's feelings for the plight of the black man is revealed in this first novel, which can be read as either proslavery or antislavery. On one hand the slaves' condition in bondage is painted as a careless and happy one, and the slaveholders are generally represented as kind, humane, and indulgent. As he firmly puts the slaves "in their place" by making them stereotypical, minstrel show Black Samboes, Harben treats the slavery issue from the Southern standpoint. One character proclaims, "Is niggers to be put on the same footin' with respectable white folks?"[10] Harben has Marie frequently feel an unaccountable repugnance for the black race, shrinking from their contact. In a defense of the book to a portion of the South which compared it to "the libelous fabrications of Mrs. Stowe,"[11] Harben wrote that he was pointing out the differences between the two races: "If the Southern people were fully aware of the vast number of Northern people who believe in the inherent equality of the white and black races, few of them, at least, would object to a Southerner trying to prove such a view erroneous."[12] By his own admission, then, Harben portrayed the eternal aversion of the white to the mixing of his blood with that of the black. Illustrating the impossibility of a consolidation of the races was his admitted concern.

But perhaps Harben was merely pacifying an irate South and intended an underlying meaning not so simple as the most obvious one, for a closer reading of the story reveals a sharp condemnation of the Old South's aristocratic values. With Colonel Bickerstaff's consent, Johnson forces the gentle Marie to marry a crude slave by whom she will have mulatto children. Harben could be illustrating a savage weakness in the system: using human beings as mere breeders without personal choice of mates.[13] But the brutal cruelty of Johnson is no more detestable

than the caste prejudice of the "better" characters. Marie's
aristocratic real mother destroys her daughter's life rather than
confront the reality of her situation. Colonel Bickerstaff's
excessive family pride causes him to treat his slaves as property,
resulting in his son's death and his own eventual ruin. Thus the
horrible effects of the slave system are subtly depicted, and
Harben, whether consciously or unconsciously, becomes an
antislavery advocate.

There took place several heated arguments in newspapers and
magazines concerning *White Marie*. Some Southerners felt that
the book was a reflection on the South which had upheld the
institution of slavery, and that it would simply open up old
wounds. In a series of letters to the Atlanta *Constitution*, the
editor of a Dalton newspaper, H. A. Wrench, harshly criticized
the book as being thoroughly unrepresentative of the South and
in his own version of *White Marie*, which he offered, shifted the
responsibility from Georgia to Vermont. According to him, an
itinerant Vermont family brought the real Marie to Georgia and
forced her to marry a black slave. While admitting that the South
was responsible for such an arrangement, the editor emphasized
that the Yankee invaders were neither "average slaveholders"
nor Southern people.[14] Harben had to be disturbed because he
received such harsh criticism from the town in which he was
born and raised, but the following week he vigorously and
logically refuted Wrench's arguments about the liberties he took
in the telling of the story. Harben cited Wrench's favorable
review of "White Jane" six months earlier, in which Wrench
allowed Harben full range of literary license, and concluded that
"there is a difference between a true story and a story founded
on a story told for a true story."[15] Wrench's reply accused
Harben, "with all the importance which he flatters to himself,"
of being a fledgling writer who too zealously sought attention
and publicity.[16] The debate ended with this third letter in the
controversy.

A newspaper editorial in Knoxville, Tennessee, Harben's
adopted city, opposed *White Marie* in yet another way. The
article, a plea for beautiful, pleasant stories in the genteel
tradition, used Harben's novel as the representation of the
unpleasant, evil side of life: "The aim of all true art as of all true
living should be to help, to elevate, and there can be no elevation
in the contemplation of such offensively ugly models as nature

produces when she is not well."[17] Harben's answer argued that
the editorial wanted writers to gloss over the realities of life
because "it pains our selfish hearts to read of unpleasant things.
We would sit in our pleasant homes in comfort and not think of
the people of our kind who are dying for lack of food and
warmth. Oh, no! Only the beautiful."[18] In a solid defense, he
pointed out the absurdity of the position the editorial took.

M. C. Williams, critic for *Epoch Magazine,* saw nothing good
about the novel, which was "weak in touch, false in tone, utterly
abominable in English." He especially deplored the climax, the
forced marriage, which he felt Harben represented as habitual.[19]
One of Harben's champions, Mrs. Lee C. Harby of Charleston,
South Carolina, answered that Harben had qualified the events
Williams criticized by specifically stating, in the body of the
book, that they were of "so eccentric a nature that the author
would caution the reader against regarding them as typical of the
date and country." She concluded that Williams obviously could
not read.[20] Williams lamely defended his position by reasserting
that Harben had implied that such forced marriages were
habitual. "He may maltreat the English language to his heart's
content without let or hindrance from me, if he will only leave
alone the law and the facts of life down South in the olden days
and golden."[21] The heated exchange ended in a stalemate.

White Marie may be looked upon as a curiosity piece today.
Harben's sister Kate claimed that her brother "was never proud
of it. Fortunately it was soon out of print."[22] Whatever the
critical appraisal, it was a beginning for the novelist; and despite
his sister's remarks, he took pride in its reception: "Its success
has exceeded my highest expectations. The sale has been limited
to no section of the country. It has been read and discussed North
and South. I could write another story at once, but shall proceed
slowly and carefully with the one I have now in hand. My
purpose is not to allow the critics an opportunity of saying that I
am trying to trade on the reputation of my first book."[23]

Now permanently settled in New York, Harben continued to
write short stories to earn his living, and also started his second
novel. Always a social charmer wherever he was, he became a
popular figure in the literary world of the city during his first few
years there, especially after the success of *White Marie.* In 1890
a society columnist reported that "in person Mr. Harben is as
lithe and slender as a young pine in his native Georgian forests.

He has a beautiful and sympathetic voice, and an attractive manner, which has won him many friends in literary circles in New York this last winter. As a *raconteur,* he is notably charming, and his conversations and anecdotes are as picturesque as his literary style."[24]

II   Almost Persuaded

Harben's second novel, *Almost Persuaded,* was published in 1891. He had read the unfinished manuscript to his family on one of his visits to Dalton, where his sister Kate's criticisms and suggestions led him to dedicate it to her. Kate felt that if it had not been sold outright after a first limited edition and then been lost by the purchasing publishers who failed after buying it, "it might have achieved the popular success which Sheldon's 'In His Steps' had some years later. It had a similar theme."[25] Indeed, the book is the first of Harben's social gospel novels. He became strongly attracted to religious themes, and employed principles of Christianity as major and minor motifs in many of his novels over the next twenty years, culminating with *Jane Dawson* in 1911.

Despite some outrageous plot situations, *Almost Persuaded* is a powerful book. Harben's ideas are sound throughout, and the theological conversations, which comprise the greater part of the novel, show insights into religious problems which have bothered mankind since the beginning of Christianity. These problems were obviously Harben's own, and the conversations were his means of voicing them. His interest in them was probably the result of his youthful rebellion against the conservative religion his father had tried to force on the family when he organized the new church in Dalton. Harben's theme is the contrast between theological dogma and personal character: he strongly implies that one of the ironies of the behavior of Christians is that the love of God and the teachings of Jesus are often on the lips of professing Christians, and that in terms of ethical Christian behavior nonChristians seem to do more for their fellow men than most Christians. He builds his plot around this theme.

Henry Lawson, a refined young man of twenty-five, accepts a position in Texas from millionaire R. F. Clayton to become the companion of Clayton's son Stanley, a few years younger than Lawson. Clayton's niece Edna also lives at the secluded ranch,

and Lawson quickly sees that she is in love with her cousin
Stanley. Stanley is an enigma, a simple yet complex young man
who has the ability actually to communicate with animals. He is a
doubter, constantly questioning traditional Christian theology,
and he unsettles his family with his ideas. As a result they rebel,
close their minds, and become even more rigid in their dogmatic
beliefs. Clayton and Edna try too hard to convince Stanley of the
literal truth of the Bible, a truth Stanley cannot accept. Stanley
sees the many similarities between biblical stories and
mythological ones—"impossible ideas of heathen races," according to his father, who tries to *force* his son to acquiesce to
traditional Christianity. But Stanley cannot reconcile astronomy
and the Bible, God's knowingly creating evil in the form of the
serpent, God's having a conceivable shape or substance, and the
cruelty of sacrificing birds and animals "of a sweet savor unto the
Lord." He cannot believe in a religion through blind faith: "That
is just where I cannot understand a Christian's standpoint. . . . I
can't see how you feel that your faith in a thing should be
absolute proof of its truth."[26]

A crucial incident occurs when Edna makes an attempt at
philanthropy. She visits an impoverished young man who is losing
his sight and needs five hundred dollars to have it corrected.
When she raises only one hundred dollars, she buys a new carpet
for the local church with the money. Stanley is enraged at her
act, and with Lawson goes to the local banker and persuades him
to help raise more than the required amount. Lawson is
extremely impressed with the effectiveness of Stanley's deed
and with the purity of his thoughts. When he tells Clayton of
Stanley's work, the father, pleased, hints at a deeper secret about
Stanley, and finally reveals what had been the mystery.
Bereaved by the death of his wife many years ago, Clayton had
sought solace in travelling with his infant son, Stanley. In the
South Seas the father and son were separated by a shipwreck.
Stanley was then reared in the jungle by lions (hence his ability
to communicate with animals) and was literally a wild man when
his father found him more than eighteen years later. Clayton
took Stanley to his secluded ranch in Texas where the young
man's education and intellectual awakening began. He acquired
knowledge rapidly, and since he had not been conditioned as
most children, his views and insights into all matters were fresh
and spontaneous.

Harben's theory is that our religious beliefs are really formed for us by others, when we are too young to know anything about the process. The keen mind that Stanley possessed had never been subjected to this unconscious absorption of opinion; he had ideally grasped the true Christian doctrine of love, a doctrine most professing Christians are oblivious to.

After residing with the Claytons for a year, Lawson and his new family move to New York City, since Clayton feels that his son should be ready for the outside world. But Stanley is dumbfounded by the social injustices of the city and by the hypocrisy of the churches and their members. He sees the human misery around him and takes it upon himself to relieve every case of distress which comes to his notice. His basic theory is to cease preaching "Be good," and to practice the more sensible text, "*Do* good."

When an uncle of Lawson dies suddenly and wills him an estate in Virginia, Lawson departs, leaving the Claytons to solve their own problems. Edna will not marry Stanley unless he sees the "light" as she does, but he cannot accept her ultimatum which would impose her brand of religion on him. On his deathbed Clayton refuses to be comforted by a renowned minister who tells him of Stanley's innate goodness. To Clayton, Stanley is doomed for his inability to literally accept the divinity of Christ.

Edna and Stanley, who share equally in Clayton's fortune, part after his death. Stanley distributes his wealth in the slums of New York, relieving the needs of the ill and the starving; his share is gone within a year. Edna begins to find little satisfaction in donating to already wealthy churches and in sponsoring snobbish young men who are candidates for the ministry. Finally she realizes that Stanley is the true Christian and has thousands of followers when one of them exclaims, "He is more like Christ than any man that ever lived! . . . He will convert the world." [27] Edna joins Stanley in his charitable work, and together they prepare to go through life serving others. He has converted her.

The book would have possessed greater interest if the mystery of Stanley, carefully concealed until the twenty-first chapter, had been cleared up earlier so the reader might watch the development of a mind which for eighteen years was a blank. The story of Stanley's eighteen years with a pride of lions and of Clayton's coincidental discovery that his son is still alive is unbelievable and preposterous, yet the reader is expected to accept it unquestioningly. Henry Lawson's awkward exit from the novel is too abrupt and final, for the reader had come to see him as a major character; much of the plot focused on him and his reactions to Stanley's ideas. He was the equivalent of Henry James's "fine central intelligence," but Harben has him depart unceremoniously and he is never mentioned again.

Finally, all the characters except Stanley are wooden symbols of absolute right and wrong rather than real persons. Stanley, though, is Harben's first fully developed outsider in a novel. Marie, in *White Marie*, had been outside the normal order in a physical sense, but Stanley's beliefs—or nonbeliefs—make him intellectually different. He stands alone, apart from others, despite his logical reasoning. Perhaps he represents the coming "Disciple of Christ," though attackers of the novel believed his "mental deformities hardly make him fit to pose as the modern Messiah."[28] He is definitely a character isolated from his normal surroundings.

The reception of the novel was for the most part favorable. The review by B. O. Flower, editor of the *Arena*, who called it one of the best works to appear in recent years, is typical: "Harben voices in a most striking manner the hunger of the age, which cries for deeds rather than creeds; for life rather than profession; for works rather than dogmas."[29]

While the book has its flaws, it is a powerful tract because it forces the reader to think, to argue, to evaluate his own practices and ideas about Christian doctrines. It is a novel that Harben was proud of, especially when he went abroad for the second time several years later and Queen Victoria requested an autographed copy of the book, which could not be bought in London at the time. Harben had a copy rebound in silk and vellum, wrote his name on the title page in gold, and presented it to the queen. When the story leaked out, the demand for the book in England, where it passed through several editions, was tremendous. As a result Harben was elected an honorary member of the British literary organization, the Savage Club.[30]

III   A Mute Confessor

After the success of *Almost Persuaded*, Harben immediately began work on his third novel, again experimenting with an entirely different concept in theme and style. In the meantime, having been especially impressed with the encouragement of the

Youth's Companion, he saturated himself with the literary spirit
of the periodical and in the course of several years furnished it
with many short stories, all of which were accepted and paid for
before publication. His invitation to visit the magazine's offices in
Boston resulted in his taking an editorial desk at the *Companion*
in 1891. This appointment was one indication of the striking and
immediate success of the author, whose sudden rise to favor in
the literary world was gratifying and almost unprecedented.

Although a respected, hard-working editor at his new position,
he still found time to finish the novel he had started earlier in
New York. When *A Mute Confessor: The Romance of a Southern
Town* appeared in 1892, most critics hailed the work as Harben's
best yet. "It proves that Mr. Harben's field is widening—that he
can tell a dainty and graceful love story as well as debate a social
problem [*White Marie*] or a case of conscience [*Almost Persuaded*]."31

The plot of *A Mute Confessor* concerns Edgar Morton, a
promising, impoverished, but vain and overly ambitious young
novelist from Massachusetts who ruthlessly plans to marry
heiress Jean Wharton for her money and influence. To study the
dialects and habits of Southerners for a new book—and to escape
from Jean, whom he has come to detest—Morton goes South
under an assumed name, Marshal Dudley. In Chattanooga he
meets Irene Stanton, an unpublished young authoress, and
immediately falls in love with her, especially after a perilous
rescue scene on Lookout Mountain in which hero and heroine
cling to the edge of a cliff—and to each other.

After saving Irene's life, Morton visits the declining Stanton
estate in a small town in Georgia where he boards for several
months. As their love grows, the couple talk of literary matters,
and Irene expresses her opinion of novelist Edgar Morton, not
realizing she is speaking to Morton himself: "He has two
natures—a bad one and a good one. He moved me to tears at
times; then again I could not help despising his characters and
feeling that he had made them like himself—weak and capable
of deceit."32 Morton realizes she has categorized him exactly and
begins to feel guilty about his deception of her.

When Irene discovers Morton's real identity and his engagement to Jean, she breaks off with him completely. Miserable, he
returns to New York, where he is released from his obligation to
Jean. Yearning for Irene, Morton writes a new novel about his

love for her, assuming moral responsibilities and characteristics
in the course of the writing that he has never admitted before.
Meanwhile, Irene has written a novel of *her* feelings, which she
coincidentally sells to Morton's publishers. After each has read
the other's novel, the two budding literary greats come together
again—wiser, more understanding of each other, and more in
love than before.

Although Harben gets to the heart of universal emotions of
people in love—their joys and miseries—the novel is one of the
most hackneyed of his career. Some critics placed *A Mute
Confessor* in the Realistic mold, but Harben's endless, ponderous
descriptions of hearts desiring and breasts heaving have a
noticeably oldfashioned formality—even for 1892—that is more
appropriate for women's magazine stories than for a Realistic
novel. One reviewer stated that the story has "none of the
coarseness or blunt epigram that is so commonly mistaken for
realism," that the style is "eminently chaste, terse, and pleasing,"
and that the novel puts Harben "on a level with the finish of
Howells, the fearlessness of Garland, and the pith of Richard
Harding Davis."[33] In fact, on the basis of this book, Harben was
one of three writers—Davis and Garland were the others—to be
singled out by one critic as the possible future author of the
"Great American Novel."[34]

But melodramatic situations and overdone dialogue were
crucial to popular success then, and Harben was shrewd enough
to know that such scenes as the rescue from the precipice were
exactly what the reading public wanted. Today the scene
appears overlong, forced, and unintentionally comic in its
execution; yet this very scene was cited as one which "thrills and
stirs the reader above almost any recent realistic writing."[35]
Other situations are just as crude and abusively coincidental,
such as the wind blowing the carbon copy of Morton's letter to
Jean into Irene's hand.

Harben's portrayal of Morton—Harben himself, perhaps, with
the tinge of vanity and ambition—is rendered with truth and
sincerity, despite Morton's shortcomings and backslidings. Yet
Morton remains a wooden character because of the artificial
dialogue; Harben had not yet learned that he was more
successful in dealing with characterizations of simple, uneducated mountaineers instead of learned, aristocratic types. Irene
Stanton is the heroine of the orthodox kind, thoroughly ideal.

"She is a woman such as no woman would have drawn, for she exists nowhere on earth, save perhaps in men's hearts."[36] She shows the spark of individuality and energy common to Harben's subsequent female characters, but, like Morton, her perfection in language and manners prevents her from becoming a fully realized character.

Harben shows his appreciation of Joel Chandler Harris when he has Irene refer to "our own 'Uncle Remus.' Oh, I think Harris is grand! He gets my heartstrings in his grasp when I read his stories."[37] In the Harris tradition, all the blacks are depicted as lovable, faithful servants of the Stanton family; they especially appreciate Morton and his liberal views, for they are intrigued by a man who shows them respect and equality. But Harben makes little use of this theme here. Still, as in *White Marie,* his delineations of Uncle Tony and the other black servants on the Stanton estate are the truest and strongest sketches in the story. The sympathy and attachment existing between the family and Uncle Tony, a former slave, is delicately traced; also Uncle Tony's attempt to help his impoverished master by offering his savings rings quaintly true. Today's world would label Uncle Tony an Uncle Tom, but to deny that such devotion at one time existed would be historically inaccurate: Harben, a social historian, is recording a social truth, offensive though it may be to today's readers.

In the final analysis, *A Mute Confessor,* though a decidedly inferior work, because of its popularity as a typical light novel of the day, advanced Harben's career. He later wrote other romances which sold well, but their literary value is more questionable than his specialty, the regional novels of North Georgia.

IV   *"A Break for Liberty"*

While Harben was an editor at the *Youth's Companion,* his co-workers saw his potential for more creative literary work than the reviewing of manuscripts of others. One of the editors submitted a copy of Harben's short story "A Filial Impulse" to the *Century Magazine,* one of the best and most influential literary magazines of the day, because "the story is worthy of magazine use and of a more appreciative adult audience than the

Companion offers it."[38] Three editors of the *Century* subsequently read and thoroughly analyzed the story to evaluate its merit; all agreed to its being worthy of publication in their magazine. Opinions such as these soon prompted Harben to leave his position at the *Companion* and concentrate completely on his own work.

His experience at the magazine was invaluable because it had given him the business judgment to guide him in his dealings with editors and publishers; but after almost two years there, Harben realized that he preferred to be free to follow his inclinations rather than conform to the grinding routine of the editorial desk. In an interview, he commented, "Great Scott! I didn't want to edit other people's stories. I want to write them myself. I was with the cleanest literary set in America, but I saw that I could work there a lifetime reading and revising manuscripts and never make a reputation. So I made a break for liberty, so to speak, and you will hear from me pretty soon."[39]

In 1893 when he returned to New York briefly, his mother, who was living alone in Dalton, suffered a paralytic stroke. Since Harben was able to get away more easily than any of the married daughters, he went to Georgia for several months to devote himself to her.[40] While in Dalton, Harben was urged by his Georgia friends, including a senator and an ex-governor, to apply for a position as German consul for the state in Atlanta. Because of his extensive knowledge of the language and his acquaintance with German customs and literature, he was a serious contender for the post, but his total commitment to his literary work prompted him to withdraw from the competition.[41] However, the gesture gratified him, because it meant that any hard feelings in his home state caused by *White Marie* four years before were now disappearing.

After his mother's death in November, 1893, Harben spent almost a year in England and Europe. He passed a good deal of his time on this second trip in London, where he studied and read at the British Museum, visited his aristocratic relatives, and met leading authors and publishers. It was at this time that Queen Victoria requested a copy of *Almost Persuaded.* On his return, when questioned about the London literary life, he replied that he had seen its bright side. "They made me an honorary member of the Savage and Authors' Clubs, and of course I met all the

leading literary men and journalists. Most of them are bright and
attractive fellows socially." Thomas Hardy impressed him most
favorably:

He and DuMaurier, Anthony Hope, and Conan Doyle are in the front
rank at present. . . . Haggard and Bret Harte are not talked about
much. The realistic school of literature of the W. D. Howells type is on
its last legs over there. . . . What the French would call risque stories
seem to be in the lead in England, and I am sorry to see it. Even Hardy
writes too many of them.[42]

V   The Land of the Changing Sun

   Harben settled in New York again in 1894 after his European
trip and dove into the social life of the city, at the same time
writing diligently. One of his apprentice novels was his only
contribution to science fiction, *The Land of the Changing Sun,*
published in 1894. This imaginative work, written in the Jules
Verne fashion, is one of the most entertaining of his books.
Vernon Louis Parrington, Jr., cites the novel as typical of escape
literature of the 1890s which used the utopian framework. In his
opinion, it "shows imagination and vigor; it has some rousing
action and a pleasant enough love story. . . . As utopian novels
go, this is extremely readable."[43]
   Two aeronauts, Charles Thorndyke, an Englishman, and Harry
Johnston, an American, land their damaged balloon on an
uncharted, deserted island in the Atlantic. Soon they are taken
prisoners by the crew of a submarine which surfaces on a lake.
After reaching the bowels of the earth via the submarine,
spaceships, and elevators, the prisoners reach a vast eternal
kingdom, Alpha, which is lighted by an electric sun. Alpha had
been discovered generations before by shipwrecked sailors who
had approved the healthful air in the huge caves and had
migrated within the earth and set up a new order of government.
The Alphians are perfect physical specimens, but this perfection
is achieved by a drastic policy: the unhealthy or "tainted" are
isolated behind a great wall and left to starve.
   Thorndyke and Johnston are given ultra-modern physical
examinations, which reveal that Thorndyke is in perfect shape
but that Johnston lacks the physical perfection required to live in
Alpha. He is taken to the wasteland territory beyond the great

wall, where he is abandoned. But he and Branasko, an Alphian he meets there, manage to escape after many harrowing experiences.

In the meantime Thorndyke, after ingratiating himself with the king by his wit and candor, falls in love with the king's daughter, Bernardino, who tries to aid her lover in finding Johnston again. Johnston and Branasko finally join Thorndyke and Bernardino and reveal their discovery that the sea has broken into the earth and will cause great explosions in Alpha when the water reaches the internal fires. In a truly exciting climax, the catastrophe is postponed; preparations are made to abandon the utopia within two years, return to the outside world, and start a new government.

The Land of the Changing Sun is well constructed and vividly written. After the two aeronauts are separated, Harben takes up the adventures of each in alternating chapters, finally reuniting them again in the end. This device allows his imagination free rein, since he can then describe both the perils (Johnston's adventures) and the delights (Thorndyke's experiences) of the underground kingdom. The two major characters are effectively contrasted. Thorndyke is a witty, carefree, unexcitable hero, while Johnston is serious, pessimistic, and highly excitable. Both are courageous men, the constant juxtaposition of whose personalities adds to the interest and complexity of the novel. Princess Bernardino is the typical romantic heroine, beautiful and willing to do anything to help her lover. Though taught nothing of God and the Christian religion, in the end, as the kingdom awaits annihilation, she intuitively begins to pray in a sort of religious frenzy. Her actions seem to attempt a rather forced moral lesson that Alpha is not a utopia without Christianity.

Social problems and reforms are hinted at by Harben in the course of the rapidly paced excitement, sometimes interfering with the otherwise neat construction of the novel. As he had shown in *Almost Persuaded,* Harben was acutely aware of social injustices. The social criticism is clear in Bernardino's concept of the outside world she has never seen: "I have heard little about your world except that your people are discontented, weak and insane, and that your changeable weather and your careless laws regarding marriage and heredity produce perpetual and innum-

erable diseases; that your people are not well developed and
beautiful; that you war with one another, and that one tears
down what another builds."[44]

In contrast, the success of Alpha is explained by the king as he
discusses the goodness of his world as opposed to the evils of the
earth:

Generation after generation we improve mentally and physically. We
are the only people who have ever attempted to thoroughly study the
science of living. Your medical men may be numbered by the millions;
your remedies for your ills change daily; what you say is good for the
health today is tomorrow believed to be poison; today you try to make
blood to give you strength, and half a century ago you believed in
taking it from the weakest of your patients. With all this fuss over
health, you will think nothing of allowing the son of a man who died of a
loathesome disease to marry a woman whose family has never had a
taint of blood. Here no such thing is thought of. To begin with, no
person who is not thoroughly sound can remain with us. Every heart
beat is heard by our medical men and every vein is transparent. You see
evidence of our system in the men and women around you.[45]

Though Harben indirectly urges a better health program in the
world, Parrington maintains that the terms on which Harben
would secure this perfect race are much too severe. "And it is
the terms which are important, for all reforms must be based
essentially on compromise."[46]

The Boston *Courier* wrote that it would be stranger than the
story itself if *The Land of the Changing Sun* did not "plow a deep
furrow in the field of imaginative literature."[47] Claude R. Flory
uses the novel as an example of the utopian novel as a peculiar
continuation of Romanticism, and concludes that it is "frankly an
extravaganza, but has some good dramatic moments."[48] Kenneth
M. Roemer sees it as a prophetic work in which Harben suggests
intrinsic dangers associated with technological progress: *"The
Land of the Changing Sun* clearly demonstrates that in the year
of Huxley's birth and a full nine years before Orwell's birth at
least one American author had had a glimpse of Big Brother and
the brave new world, a glimpse of 1984 in 1894."[49]

The book is so thoroughly enjoyable and well written that it is
puzzling why Harben never attempted another science-fiction
novel. But he was still searching for the key to public taste.

VI *Journalistic Jesting; Marriage*

During the 1890s Harben syndicated to Southern newspapers a weekly column about the literary gossip of New York, "fresh and racy articles about the bohemian life of the metropolis."[50] A close literary friend, poet-columnist Frank L. Stanton, was writing his "Just from Georgia" column for the Atlanta *Constitution* at the same time. Both men were fond of practical jokes and used their respective columns to let thousands of readers share in their whimsy. Readers of Stanton's column noticed his frequent good-natured jokes on Harben throughout the years. For example, while Harben was vacationing in Europe, Stanton had the novelist dining with the Prince of Wales, being robbed in the Black Forest, on the point of marrying a wealthy Russian countess, and fighting a duel in Paris with a citizen who had assailed one of his books. Harben won the duel because he "used the Georgia shotgun, which played such havoc with the wild animals of the Cohutta Mountains when the now-celebrated novelist was a humble moonshiner in the Empire State of the South."[51] Even though Harben knew the value of such unsolicited publicity, he could not remain silent. In one of his syndicated letters he had Stanton "talking up the interests of his Atlanta Orphan Asylum. Mr. Stanton has conceived the praiseworthy idea of building a home for the orphan children of poor Southern editors, and has already received enough encouragement to believe that this plan will eventually be successful."[52] Not a word of truth was in it, but Harben's column was copied in five hundred American newspapers. The result was that Stanton was inundated with letters from widows and orphans all over the United States, begging to know when his asylum would be open. Both writers had had their fun, and Stanton finally admitted that his practical jokes had been matched. But he delivered a final thrust by fabricating an editor's answer on why Harben's accepted stories had not appeared in the editor's magazine: " 'There is a conspiracy here to hold them until you are dead, as they would naturally have greater interest then. How is your health?' Harben tore the note to tatters and got married."[53]

Indeed, during the summer of 1896, when he was almost thirty-eight years of age, Harben made one of his frequent visits

to Dalton and found the perfect woman he had been seeking for
so long. In the course of a five-week whirlwind courtship, he
met, wooed, and won Miss Maybelle Chandler of Kingstree,
South Carolina, who was a summer visitor with a neighbor of the
Harbens. Maybelle, descended from one of the oldest and most
aristocratic families of South Carolina, was thus described in
their somewhat flowery newspaper announcement: "She is
exquisitely beautiful; has large black eyes; graceful, lithe, and
only seventeen years old. Her father, Joe Chandler, was a
schoolmate of Mr. Harben nineteen years ago."[54] Their wedding,
which took place on July 2, 1896, at the home of a friend, was a
quiet one with only the families present. But the marriage
created an immense surprise; a large crowd gathered at the train
to speed them on their honeymoon journey. "All congratulate
them, him on winning a pearl of great price, her on winning one
of the South's brainiest sons, for whom a bright future lies in
store."[55]

Harben's sister Kate reported that the marriage was an
unquestioned success, that her brother's romantic wanderings
ended after he met Maybelle. "She was always his true mate,
helper, and beautiful inspiration, willing to sacrifice of her
budding youth in order to meet him more than half way on the
path of his life's ambition, finding her pleasure in his literary
circle and her music, rather than in the dance of gaiety to which
youth and beauty entitled her."[56]

A daughter of Harben's sister Frances lived in France. As a
wedding present to Harben and his bride the niece invited the
newlyweds to Paris for a visit. Robert Loveman accompanied the
couple, when the sense of humor of the two writers was once
again in evidence. Finding it almost impossible to go through the
Louvre without being bothered by guides, the two friends solved
the problem by pretending to speak only Choctaw, since the
guides seemed to know every other language. Harben's wife
reported that when a guide approached, Harben and Loveman
"looked dumb and mumbled incomprehensible guttural syllables
ending with 'um aah Choctaw.' I remained silent. Soon the guides
gave up and we strolled unmolested through the halls viewing
the art treasures."[57]

After their Parisian visit the couple "gypsied on the conti-
nent," visiting Germany, Switzerland, and Holland, before they
began to long to hear English spoken again. They mixed

sightseeing, social life, and business in their trip to London, spending much time at the home of the author of *Little Lord Fauntleroy*, Frances Hodgson Burnett, whom Harben had known in Boston. Maybelle especially impressed the Britishers with her simple, flat, Southern way of talking.[58] The Harbens made occasional trips to England in later years, where the demands for his work made it necessary to live periodically to protect his foreign copyright.

The couple made their permanent home in New York City, though they spent part of every summer in Dalton. Here Harben and Loveman loafed together, roamed the hills, sat in stores whittling and absorbing the mountain stories, and studied at first hand the kinds of people Harben made famous. Harben's analysis did not stop at the stores and streets; he sought out the mountaineers in their homes and tramped over the hills with them, gathering material for his books. But his experimental period was not yet over, and the next genre he undertook was detective fiction.

VII   *The Detective Novels*

Arthur Conan Doyle's famous character Sherlock Holmes, who was patterned after Edgar Allan Poe's C. Auguste Dupin, was the rage at the time. Harben must have studied Doyle's and Poe's works faithfully, for his next novels were detective stories with striking similarities to such tales of ratiocination. Harben used such elements as the scholarly, sophisticated sleuth, the worshipful stooge, the stupid police officers, the simple clues, and the careful working-out of the problem. The detective tales of Poe, Doyle, and Harben are simply means of setting up logical conditions and then pursuing them to their results.

Like Dupin and Holmes, Harben's detective, Minard Hendricks, is a learned gentleman of leisure; he is eccentric, appearing to be almost stupid as he analyzes and absorbs the clues of each case he is solving. Just as Dupin is balanced by the narrator of the Poe story and Holmes by Dr. Watson, Minard Hendricks needs to be balanced by a man of average intelligence who functions as the link between the detective and the reader. Hendricks's confidant is Dr. Henry Lampkin, a medical doctor and famous hypnotic expert, to whom Hendricks must carefully explain the meaning of the clues. As Dr. Lampkin is enlightened, so is the reader, and the brilliant wisdom of Hendricks is also celebrated. Just as Dupin and Holmes are looked upon with pride and awe by their respective police authorities, Hendricks is respected—almost revered—by police forces throughout the country, who invite the detective to bring his own method to the solution of the crimes which have them baffled. Hendricks intuitively sets aside the trivia, puts the essential facts together, and proves by deduction and induction that his solution is the only logical one.[59]

America's introduction to Minard Hendricks came in "From Clue to Climax." This short novel was never published in book form, but it appeared as the lead story in the June 1896 issue of *Lippincott's Monthly Magazine*. In an unnamed American city, Hendricks is called to help solve the mysterious death of a wealthy banker who is found murdered with a ghastly smile on his face, as though he had been in a trance when killed. Hendricks joins forces with Dr. Lampkin, whose expertise in hypnosis helps the detective find the killer, a mentally unbalanced hypnotist.

In "From Clue to Climax," a run-of-the-mill detective story containing all the characteristics of a Poe-Doyle tale, Harben firmly establishes the basic qualities of Hendricks. Hendricks's intense preoccupation with pondering the clues as they are presented to him is mistaken for stupidity: "That man must be overrated, certainly. If I had not heard that he was a brilliant member of his profession, I should have said he was the most stupid man alive. I was so irritated by his dawdling actions that I was tempted to turn my back on him." Dr. Lampkin later explains, "He has been discharged from more than one case for looking like an idiot, but that's part of his method. He knows what he is doing."[60]

In 1898 Harben's second detective novel was published. *The Caruthers Affair* is superior to "From Clue to Climax" in several respects. Although the outcome is predictable to most mystery fans, it is a well-constructed, suspenseful story with a more careful arrangement of clues, none of which miss the perceptive eyes of Minard Hendricks. The startling incidents rush along. Harben's style is smooth, forceful, and graphic—definitely more readable than his previous efforts; his abilities as a writer show a marked improvement. The dialogue and descriptions are far more natural than ever before. Minard Hendricks is notified of a murder by the killer himself, who dares the detective to find the body *and* the killer. When Hendricks easily finds the cremated body, the remainder of the plot centers on his tracking down the killer with the aid of Dr. Lampkin (whose hypnotic expertise comes in handy once again) in spite of the hindrances of "that blockhead Denham," the obligatory stupid policeman.

The novel, which Harben dedicated to Lord and Lady Harben of England, never lags. Dr. Lampkin's slow witted enlightenment is again a chief characteristic of the story: "Lampkin was speechless with surprise. He had been slow to grasp the awful seriousness of their predicament, but when he did it completely unnerved him." And Hendricks's extraordinary cleverness is once more in evidence throughout the novel, usually in Dr. Lampkin's praise of him: "My friend, my pride in you is as boundless as interstellar space. You are more than a detective— you are an histrionic genius."[61]

Insofar as several of Harben's rural characters in later works are amateur detectives, he obviously enjoyed writing such tales.[62] The careful construction and readable style of the works prove that, as in all his endeavors so far, he was more than moderately successful.

The decade of the 1890s was a transitional period in American literature. The different types of novels Harben wrote during these years mirror a wide range of literary preference in America. Most of the novels were modeled after contemporary popular works. So, except for his short stories, Harben had not fully tapped his knowledge of the Georgia region he knew best. His next book-length publication, *Northern Georgia Sketches,* was a collection of his best short stories, and was the work responsible for his concentration on the regional novels for which he became critically as well as popularly recognized.

CHAPTER 3

The Short Stories

HARBEN began his literary career by writing short stories; he was especially prolific in this genre during the 1890s and was an extremely popular contributor to current periodicals of the day. The New York *Times* reported, "In glancing over the contents of a magazine there has always been pleasure in finding the title of a story by Mr. Harben."[1] Although he experimented with different types of novels in this decade, most of his short stories were local-color sketches about his own North Georgia region, depicting the character types and social conditions of the area he knew well. With only a few exceptions, he wisely avoided stories of aristocrats, whom he never was able to portray successfully; his tales are accurate foreshadowings of and unconscious preparations for his later regional novels.

Harben's North Georgia people, unlike the romantic Creoles of George Washington Cable or the remote mountaineers of Mary Noailles Murfree, are closer to the types found in the fiction of fellow Georgians Judge Augustus Baldwin Longstreet, Richard Malcolm Johnston, and Joel Chandler Harris, all of whose works Harben knew. In the treatment of his characters, black and white, Harben is less inclined toward the idyllic than most writers of the mountains. Usually his whites are poor people. But to consider them "poor white trash" is misleading. They are, rather, poor yeoman farmers—religious, gregarious, and independent—but rarely irresponsible, shiftless, or depraved.[2] Their atmosphere is secure and stable. They are sociable people, gathering in small groups at the country stores and quilting bees and in larger assemblies at camp meetings and corn-shuckings, acting out of the combined motives of duty and pleasure. The problems caused by the freeing from slavery of the blacks, still fresh in the minds of Southerners, provided Harben with a basis for commentary on both Southern blacks and whites.

Harben's paternalistic racial attitude was prevalent in his day, but even when he is slightly condescending toward them, he portrays blacks realistically and lovingly. They emerge as noble, proud individuals.

Though many of his gently ironic tales appear to be pointless, Harben was content to merely spin yarns about the people and the land he knew best. Frequently he did not capitalize on the potential impact of his material, and his resolutions are sometimes weak; but his talent lay in characterization, not plots with trick conclusions, to which end he succeeded admirably. Most of the stories are dialect sketches. Harben became expert at reproducing the speech of Georgia mountaineers and Southern blacks. At times the result is a kind of perverted and misspelled jargon, but no more so than the acclaimed dialect writings of Mark Twain and Joel Chandler Harris. Since he was a native of the mountains, Harben made the crude speech accurate and convincing. The dialects are precise examples of Southern vernacular, which he labored over painstakingly, ever inspecting the proofs of his dialect stories to assure their accuracy.[3] In 1893 his tendency toward showmanship revealed itself again in his public readings of some of the black and "cracker" dialect tales he presented. He was even offered a reading tour of Canada, but refused it since he was too busy writing.[4]

I *The Magazine Stories*

The first short story by Harben to appear in a national magazine was "The Tragic Story of Sunset Rock, Tennessee," originally published in the Chattanooga *Times* and reprinted in *Current Literature* in 1888. It is an undistinguished piece of maudlin sentimentality, but its construction is interesting. Harben's framework is the "box structure" of Southwestern humor stories, in which an educated narrator opens and closes the story. The bulk of it is told in the uneducated dialect of a character. This narrator tells of a chance meeting at Chattanooga, Tennessee, with an old man who then, in dialect, relates the story of how Sunset Rock acquired its name. In fact, he had named it years ago, after a young neighbor jumped from the rock and killed herself because of unrequited love. After the narrator leaves the spot, the grass beneath his feet "shed tears of newly born dew, as if weeping for the tragedy of twenty years before."[5]

The story is a good indication of the progress Harben had to make before he would become adept at writing fiction.

Beginning with "White Jane," printed in July, 1889, Harben wrote a long series of short stories for the *Youth's Companion* between 1889 and 1892. "White Jane" amounts to an outline of *White Marie*—which expands on the short story—but there are several noticeable differences. Unlike Marie, Jane is not an educated girl and speaks in a black dialect throughout the story. There is no hint of romantic interest with the slaveholder's son. Harben focuses on Jane's despair at being forced to marry the black slave Jake—there is actually more about her married life in the very short tale than appears in the novel. The story's theme of miscegenation created a small controversy for the youth oriented magazine, but this did not prevent the editors from accepting many more of Harben's stories over the next three years.

"John Bartow," the lead story in the September 5, 1889, issue of the *Companion*, is the familiar tale of the teenage boy who resents his widowed mother's marrying again. After she weds Duke Sanders, John leaves the Georgia hills for Texas, where he becomes a successful businessman. Fifteen years later he reads that "Mrs. Duke Sanders" has died; but when he returns to Georgia, he discovers that the newspaper had made a typographical error and that it is actually his stepfather who is dead. The mother and son are happily reunited. The chief fault of this short tale is that although Harben uses enough material to encompass a complete novel, none of it is sufficiently developed.

Harben frequently used the death of a character to create pathos in his stories. "A Message from the Stream," published in the *Youth's Companion* in October, 1889, is a sketch about a moonshiner whose wife's dying words are a plea for him to give up his illegal profession. After her death their son smells the aroma of whiskey in the brook coming from his father's moonshine cave—the "message from the stream" of the title, indicating that the father has repented. "Martha" (*Youth's Companion*, December, 1889) is an overly sentimental story about a mountain girl's marriage to the village drunkard, who kills her one night in a drunken rage and then accidentally drowns himself. The only merit in the tale is the genuine suffering of Martha's parents over their ill-fated daughter.

In "Jacob Ladd's Change of Heart" (*Youth's Companion*,

October, 1891), farmer Ladd's coldness has caused his only son to run away. Ladd and the White Caps (an early version of the Ku Klux Klan) are about to hang an innocent young man on circumstantial murder evidence when Ladd discovers that the boy has come to tell him that his son is now dead. Ladd persuades the mob to release the youth, takes him home, and gives him his dead son's clothes and a new horse in attempting to atone for his former harshness. "Fred's Mother" (*Youth's Companion*, April, 1892) concerns a youth who goes to prison for stealing a wealthy planter's money and then saves the man's life two years later, killing himself in the process. The story focuses on the boy's mother and her reactions to her son's misfortunes. "A Touch of Nature" (*Youth's Companion*, December, 1892) centers on a group of vindictive country women who hate a crotchety neighbor until the day they hear that her son has been killed in a sawmill explosion. They realize they have been cruel to her, tell her so, and are as happy as she when they discover that the report of the boy's death was an error and that he is still alive and well.

Three of Harben's stories concerning life among the blacks also appeared in the *Youth's Companion:* "Aunt Milly's Surprise" (October, 1890), "Aunt Nelly's Visit" (December, 1890), and "Aunt Dilsey's Son" (June, 1892). In the first, an impoverished old planter reunites Aunt Milly, one of his slaves, with her husband Judas, who had been separated from her for fifteen years. "Aunt Nelly's Visit" is a more interesting yarn about a black mammy who "sighed for the good times of bondage" because "to her mind, the abolition of slavery was a cruel wrong. Her master had been almost a king in her eyes, and his children princes and princesses."[6] Aunt Nelly leaves her husband, Uncle Aaron, to be with her recently married "young mistress" in New York. She is miserable in the city and learns that her place is with Aaron, to whom she returns. "Aunt Dilsey's Son" tells of an eccentric old black woman who discovers that her son, who had been sold as a child, is still alive; though she cannot afford to, she sends him money. But when he visits her and sees her state of poverty, he confesses that he is a fraud and that he had merely wanted more money. He finds a regular job and makes his home with her while she continues to pretend that he is her own son.

During the 1890s Harben became a frequent contributor to the *Independent,* the influential New York-based periodical, as well as to the *Youth's Companion.* His first story for the *Independent,* "A Dog's Role" (January, 1890), is not among his best; it is contrived, maudlin, and overlong. Dissolute tramp Edward Gilbert, returning to the Georgia town he had abandoned twenty-five years before, is first arrested for vagrancy, then hospitalized for malnutrition. His faithful dog Tige instinctively seeks out his master's brother Jasper, the mayor of the town, who readily takes in the dog. Tige leads Jasper to Edward, the brothers are happily and tearfully reunited, and the dog benefits abundantly.

"Ring Joe," published in the April, 1890, issue of the *Independent,* reappeared in November of the same year in *Short Stories* as "The Story of Ring Joe." The title character is a slovenly, thirty-year-old outcast who, despite his intellectual superiority to his peers, is ridiculed for being an ugly eccentric. When Annie Wiggins, a pretty neighbor, finally declares her admiration for him, he begins to improve his personal appearance and actions. Joe and Annie are married and in several years have two children. Then Annie sickens and dies. After agonizing months, Joe is urged to marry an older widow. On their first night at Joe's home, he is so tortured by the memory of Annie that he finally leaves his new wife, takes his children to his sister, and promptly dies of heartbreak. Everything leads nowhere, and the ending of an otherwise effective story is ridiculously weak.

Three *Independent* stories concern wayward but contrite mountaineers. "The Maltby's Son" (January, 1891) is heavy-drinking, teenage Troy, who eventually deserts his debt ridden family—to return four years later a mature, sober young man. In "Gid Sebastian's Probation" (June, 1891), the title character, a former drunkard, serves fifteen years of a life imprisonment sentence, is paroled and reunited with his wife and daughter. He is soon tempted with a bottle of moonshine whiskey which he has irrationally bought; but when he overcomes his temptation, he is sure he is on the road to full recovery. "A Mother's Verdict" (October, 1891) concerns a young man sentenced to be hanged. His mother arranges his escape from prison and then learns that the governor has granted him a full pardon. None of these three stories succeeds, primarily because of the tearfully artificial emotion Harben attempts to evoke.

Perhaps it was such offensive sentimentality that caused the proprietor of the *Independent* to give orders that not another line from "that author" be allowed in his periodical. Literary gossip reported that the magazine's editor, recognizing Harben's potential merit, urged Harben to use a fictitious name for his next piece for the *Independent*. So that his friends in the South might identify his works, he chose the name of his native town and county, Dalton and Whitfield.[7] Thus "The Elixir," by "Dalton Whitfield," appeared in the pages of the *Independent* in February, 1894. It is a confusing science-fiction yarn that should have indicated to Harben that in short fiction he was more effective when writing of people and situations to which he was close. "The Elixir" is about a scientist who discovers a drug which prolongs life indefinitely. Public revelation of the drug causes everyone to live unlimited years; population increases drastically, crime runs rampant. After many years, the now ancient scientist rescinds his elixir, and the story ends hopefully, simply because people begin dying again.

The proprietor of the *Independent* obviously followed the ancient scientist's lead and rescinded his refusal to allow a Harben story in his magazine, for, in December, 1896, one more story by Harben appeared. "Two Points of View" offers a conversation between a young man and his lady friend, both unnamed. Attempting to persuade her to marry him rather than a rival, he presents himself in an honorable light by confessing knowledge of a criminal scheme which he eventually turned down. The woman fails to share his viewpoint, however; in fact, she punctures his story by pointing out inconsistencies which show him to be not only dishonorable but dishonest before firmly rejecting him. The story is a complete reversal of Harben's usual method—strong story, weak conclusion. This time the situation is overly sentimental until the ironic, unexpected twist at the end, which saves the sketch.

Harben did not confine himself to writing solely for the *Youth's Companion* and the *Independent*. His stories appeared in such notable magazines as *Lippincott's, Century, Harper's Monthly, Ladies' Home Journal, Woman's Home Companion, Short Stories, Arena, Book News,* and *Outlook*. He was especially proud of his association with the more prestigious periodicals, for in a letter to Richard Watson Gilder, editor of the *Century Magazine,* he stated, "I'd rather have a bare chance of seeing it in the *Century* in the far future than to sell it elsewhere for immediate use. The best critics all over America are saying that my Southern types and studies are highly worthy, and it makes me *sick* to see them presented in any but the highest magazines."[8]

The following stories are representative of those which appeared in the magazines listed above, as well as in others. "Two Wanderers," a story written especially for the Christmas, 1890, issue of the Atlanta-based *Dixie*, is another sketch with stereotypical, unreal characters. A dance hall in a disreputable section of New York City is inhabited by jaded, soulless men and women. When a stranger from San Francisco enters, feeling he has never sunk so low, a dejected, obviously ill ten-cents-a-dance woman begins to talk with him. As they confess their past sins, they discover that they are brother and sister, long since parted. The story ends by their visiting their aged mother in Virginia, where "they found rest and peace, did the wanderers."[9] The stilted dialogue and the illogical situation make for an inferior piece of writing, but one which reflected the taste of the American reading public for unabashed sentimentality.

"The Frog-Boy" is a promising premise gone astray by way of the same mawkish sentimentality. A completely deformed black boy, the size of an infant and resembling a frog, is kept in isolation by his mother for years, until, kidnapped and made the main freak attraction in a side show, he is befriended by the equally lonely fat lady. The sudden change in environment is too much for the delicate freak. As he is dying, the fat lady forces the proprietor to return the frog-boy's body to his home for burial. "When she looked at him again a moment later, a little white soul had escaped from the ebon mass. An invisible brush had painted triumph upon the black rigid features."[10] The story is an inferior piece in all respects because of such artificial pathos.

But pathos was Harben's specialty at the time, and his etching "Her Children" won for him the prize for Most Pathetic Etching in a national contest conducted by *Short Stories* in 1891.[11] "Her Children" is, indeed, a strangely moving one-page vignette. A gentle mother dies, leaving her equally sensitive twin boys to the care of their cruel father. The day after her burial, the boys are beaten by their drunken father. They decide to join their mother in heaven by drowning themselves "just as Father drowned our kitten in the creek." Afraid at first, the boys enter the brook, "and the moon alone saw the dark waters receive them."[12]

Perhaps because he was forced to be brief, Harben actually succeeded in creating genuine pathos in this instance.

Another powerful one-page etching of the torture and sorrow that result from the loss of one's faith is "Jim Knew," an account of a devout old mountain woman whose religion is her sole comfort. Her son Jim, returned from the West, confidently informs her that the Bible is not true, is not the inspired word of God. "Jim knew, he was always right; she had never known him to be wrong." The old woman stops attending church and soon becomes ill. As she is dying and her pastor asks her if she is prepared for death, she replies, " 'I don't know. . . . I've heerd 'at the Bible ain't true. I use ter b'lieve 'at when my time come I'd go off easy, but now it's jest awful—awful!' . . . She tried to put out her hand toward Jim, essayed to speak, but death froze her unasked question on her face."[13] The etching is effective because of its restrained, tense dialogue and because of the tortured emotions of both the old woman and her son at the end; each is equally confused and in agony.

A popular piece when it appeared in the *Arena* in September, 1891, was "He Came and Went Again," an awkwardly written story with excessively reverent clichés and ideas. Obviously an offspring of *Almost Persuaded*, published the year before, the parable concerns the reappearance of Christ in contemporary New York. He is saddened and disgusted, as before, at the lack of charity among self-proclaimed Christians; at the impatience and snobbishness of ministers who think only in terms of materialism; and at the emphasis on vanity, pride, lust, and ostentation rather than on humility, love, unselfishness, and justice. Harben's modern Jesus dies at the end, giving his last piece of bread to another starving man. Properly handled, the story could have been powerful; as it is, Harben's blatantly devout preaching and "fine" writing render it worthless.

A justifiably popular tale was "Not a Child Born," more a doomsday essay than a short story with characters. The strange discovery in 1900 that children have completely ceased to be born affects the entire world, though the story focuses on New York City. For the next hundred years, "fear and human love grew. The world was becoming inured to the idea of human extinction." The last person in the world dies as the year 2000 dawns, "but not an eye was awake to behold it."[14] The short sketch is imaginative and effective; it indicates Harben's versatility as a teller of different types of stories.

"A Cohutta Valley Shooting Match" is a slight but charming story of the ways of Georgia mountaineers. Abrum Bagley's intense dislike of Dick Martin is displayed at a corn-shucking, where young Martin wins a kiss from his sweetheart, Melissa Bagley, Abrum's daughter. After being insulted by Bagley, Martin determines to impress the older man by triumphing over Bagley's arch rival in the annual shooting match. Martin practices for a month and easily wins the match, Bagley's gratitude for bettering his rival, and the hand of Melissa. The interest in the story lies in the dialogue and the local-color spirit of the descriptions of the shooting match, especially the corn-shucking. "The rule on this occasion shall be as common, in regard to the fust feller that finds a red yeer o' corn bein' 'lowed to kiss any gal he likes, but atter that one time—understand everbody—atter that no bussin' kin take place, red yeer ur no red yeer. I advocate moderation in all things, especially whar' a man an' woman's mouth is concerned."[15]

In "Thicker Than Water" (Book News, November, 1893), Harben returned to his old theme of miscegenation, but this time on a more deliberate plane. Bostonian Leon Fincher marries a refined mulatto girl and goes off with her to the squalid Southern cabin where her people live. In the course of several years he narrowly escapes lynching, sees their black baby die, and becomes an outcast. When his wife dies he returns to Boston to resume his relationship with his former fiancée; but when she completely rejects him, as the rest of his family has, he wanders the streets a lonely and despised man. The story gives another indication of Harben's mixed feelings on racial issues. The reader, depending on his outlook, could sympathize with Fincher for his liberal views and his following his heart instead of his intellect, or condemn him for his stupidity and hindsight. After White Marie and this story, Harben tried to avoid such controversial plots concerning miscegenation.

"Br'er Cato's Power" (Chaperone, December, 1891), Harben's attempt to capture the fever and atmosphere of black church meetings, is an inferior piece. Intending to give such services respect and sincerity, he makes them comical and almost lewd instead. Br'er Cato Ashmore is a leader in his church community because of his abilities to go into either a trance or a religious frenzy on cue. When an old woman dies suddenly during one of his performances, Cato somehow feels guilty and withdraws from church functions for a full year. He finally tells his story to a new preacher, who convinces him that God would never hold him responsible for the woman's death. Cato becomes a devout Christian from then on, relinquishing his theatrical ways. "The Duel at Frog Hollow" (*Short Stories*, August, 1892) is a sluggish sketch about a duel, "jes lak der white folk," between two black men. When the two friends acting as seconds for the feuding pair substitute blank cartridges for real bullets in the duelling pistols, and after the duellers have apparently missed each other, they are satisfied that their honor and bravery have been upheld. shake hands and become friends again.

A delightfully comic view of life among the blacks is "Abrum, Ca'line and Asphalt," first published as "The Matrimonial Troubles of Abraham and Caroline" in a short lived Nashville weekly, *Round Table*, in May, 1890, and republished in *Short Stories* a year later. After describing the fierce competition between Methodists and Baptists in the village of Crippletown, Harben focuses on the devout Methodist Abraham Wilson, his "on the fence" wife Caroline, and their child Asphalt, who had been born when Abrum was employed in laying asphalt pavement in the city. Abrum was impressed with the name, which had " 'des enough pitch in it fer er nigger child's name." Ca'line's parents had been Baptists, and "from childhood up she had looked forward to immersion with as much anticipation as she had to marriage. Regardless of this she had married a Methodist, because she had loved him." Yet she doesn't want the preacher to "des sprinkle my haid out'n er gravy bowl, same as I does w'en I's ironin'." She finally decides to become a Baptist and begins taking lessons from the Baptist preacher on "w'en ter hol' my bref ter keep from stranglin'." When the resulting dissension between the couple leads to talk of divorce, Abrum sneaks his clothing, piece by piece, out of the house over a period of three weeks. Finally, on the night Abrum has reluctantly decided to leave forever, Asphalt becomes temporarily ill and the couple is reunited through the love of their child. Ca'line decides to join her husband's church because "who knows but er gwine in der water wid wet clothes might er been my regular death?"[16] The mixture of irreverence and understanding makes this story one of Harben's most enchanting.

A story which is concerned neither with mountaineers nor

blacks is "In the Year Ten Thousand," an imaginative sketch in
which Harben peers into the future. There is no plot, and the
sketch amounts to an essay on the foibles of man. In 10,000 A.D.,
a six-hundred-year-old man explains the past to a young boy as
they walk through a museum. At a time when thought reading is
a common practice, the boy is astounded that man at one time
read unattractive, useless books. Physical appearances have
changed, and the boy is disgusted to see pictures of man in 2,000
A.D. when "human beings . . . bore a nearer resemblance to the
lower animals than we do now."[17] The wrongs of capital
punishment, the spiritual genius of Jesus, the folly of wars, the
degrading consumption of flesh, the progress of the science of
mind reading, and the eventual common language and brotherly
love of the world are all discussed by the two inhabitants of the
future.

"Before Two Altars" (May, June, 1893), one of several stories
to appear in the *Ladies' Home Journal,* is an inferior effort in two
installments. The happy marriage of newlyweds Martha and
Dick Blumer ends in tragedy when Dick is killed in an accident.
Martha refuses to consent to her father's insistence that she
marry his original first choice, and leaps from a cliff to join her
dead husband. While the mountain dialect and characterizations
are realistic, the story itself is trite.

Harben took obvious delight in his use of dialects in "A
Prophet Without Honor," in which he combines his expertise in
the German language with his ear for the speech of the North
Georgia mountaineer. The appealing little story is evidently
based on Harben's real-life relationship with Mr. Knorr, the
German immigrant in Dalton who influenced his study of
German. Abe Watts, teenage son of an ignorant mountain couple,
befriends Hans Bleicher, an immigrant from Germany. Hans
confides to Abe that he is purchasing land for a colony of rich
German families who will be coming to the area in several
months. Since Hans wants Abe to become the overseer of the
colony, he teaches the boy the German language, though Abe is
ridiculed by his mountain neighbors. When Hans is bitten by a
rattlesnake and cannot make himself understood by the citizens,
the boy saves the "furriner" through his knowledge of German.
The community sees the value of a second language and becomes
proud of their "local boy made good," who moves his family from
their shack to a new plantation. Both German and mountain

dialects are excellent, and the superstitions and prejudices of the mountain people are rendered valid and realistic.

"Matt Digby's Meddling" is a touching story of how the spitefulness and interference of one person can color and prejudice an entire family against others. The meddlesome old maid Matt Digby spreads the rumor that newly married Annie McPherson is being mistreated by her older husband's grown children and is miserable. When Annie's parents are called to her bedside when she is ill, they discover that their daughter is not only very close to her new family but that she is completely happy. Annie recovers, the McPhersons realize that they have been wrongly influenced by Matt Digby, and McPherson philosophizes that "Money don't spile folks that has been well raised."[18]

"A Touch of Nature" had been an earlier Harben short story but the title reappears affixed to an essay geared to the readers of the *Outlook,* the religiously oriented magazine in which it appears. Harben tells of an experience he had encountered in Union Square in New York. A crowd of men, women, and children were desperately trying to save a sparrow which had become so drenched in the middle of a fountain that it could not fly; it was slowly dying. The citizens, who ordinarily "would have been in favor of passing a law to exterminate the entire colony of English sparrows," [19] saved the powerless one which through its helplessness taught them all a lesson. The article's purpose is the need to care for others— in this case a sparrow—but it contains no overt moralizing. Because Harben let the episode speak for itself, the essay is all the more effective for its apparent objectivity.

"A Million-Dollar Cinder" is a parable about the inherent destructive element which results from greed. Four prominent New York men know that a formula for artificially producing gold exists on a certain charred roll of paper; but every expert they call in to try to decipher the cinder fails. The men are left hopeless, nervous wrecks, having ruined their lives in search of riches. The story itself is pedestrian, but Harben's style and diction are far more natural and convincing than in other stories which do not concern mountaineers.

In 1897 and 1898, the *Woman's Home Companion* published five of Harben's stories, all about Cohutta mountaineers. In the first, "The Burial Arrangements of Elder Womack," the title character develops a morbid preoccupation with his own death, going so far as to build his own watertight coffin and digging his own grave. His wife's reaction is typical: "Ef you wuzn't a growed-up man, I'd have that coat off'n yore back, an' give you a sound lashin'."[20] His eccentricity affects the romances of both his son and daughter, until he finally relents and allows his son to destroy the coffin and fill in the grave. The story is a delightful one—full of colorful dialogue, characters, and situations—until the ineffectual ending. Harben's failure to see the possibility for a strong, ironic conclusion impairs an otherwise worthy story.

"The Shortest Road to a Man's Heart" concerns the amusing romance of a middleage couple. Marietta Barker, who made "the best pies that anybody ever put mouth to," set her cap for Hiram Castlewood; but she has a serious rival in younger Ella Worthy. Shrewdly calculating that the way to a man's heart is through his stomach, the superb cook woos Hiram with baked turkey, "hot chicken dumplin's and peach pie with sweetened cream"—and coquettishly wins him. The story is totally charming because of Marietta, a defiant country woman who is determined not to become an old maid like her counselling sister and spinster friends: "Don't you nor her nor Sallie Wilkins nor Maudie Trumble set up to teach a body how marriage is done."[21] Marietta sets up her own method and convincingly achieves her objectives.

In "On the Road to Marlet" (October, 1897), David Luttrell returns to the Cohutta Mountains after fifteen years and coincidentally meets his former sweetheart, Julia, now married to drunkard Jasper Loomis with six children. Though she and her family are in a state of abject poverty, Luttrell, who still loves her, is determined to help Julia financially. When Loomis suddenly dies, Luttrell realizes that he will be able to care for Julia and her family forever. Though the story is routine enough, Harben writes it objectively, asking for no sympathy for Julia and her situation. The tale emerges as a forthright picture of a poor country family.

"A Tie of Blood" (May, 1898) is a combination of sentimentality and realism, the former quality present in the educated dialogue of the heroine and hero, the latter in the description of the girl's lowly mountain acquaintances. Schoolteacher Elizabeth Wrenshall returns to her native hill home to be with her dying mother and wins a marriage proposal from a wealthy city banker whom she has loved for years. Perceptive descriptions of the hill people again prove to be Harben's strong point.

The fifth *Woman's Home Companion* story is a neatly ironic, superior one, "The Return of the Inconstant," in which the three main characters are true-to-life mountaineers. The power of Harben's skill in writing about hill people is in full evidence here. Joe Thornhill, an arrogantly complacent adventurer who had deserted his fiancée, Kitty Robinson, ten years before, returns "to make 'er a birthday present of my big hulkin' self." Joe boasts of his intentions to the village storekeeper, Hiram Allgood, who seems an unlikely rival in love since Hiram is shy, stout, bald, and bow-legged. The tables are turned on Joe when Kitty rejects him and accepts Hiram: "All the time he was a-talkin' I couldn't keep from thinkin' about the difference between you two. You are so good an' gentle-like, an' he's so—oh, I don't want to mention you an' him together!"[22] Harben sustains the irony throughout the story; it is one of his best.

After the turn of the century, a Harben story became a rarity in magazines of the day, for he was busy with his novels. He still wrote an occasional story, however, even after he turned to the longer form of fiction. One of them was "A Fair Exchange" (*Lippincott's*, January, 1902), set in Paris and on an ocean liner rather than in the Georgia hills. Paul Weatherford, despondent over an ill-fated love affair and determined to kill himself, first exchanges identifications with John Burlingame, a troubled friend who is trying to escape the Paris police, who want Burlingame for embezzlement. Burlingame sails for New York using Weatherford's name. When his identity is discovered he throws himself overboard and is killed. Meanwhile, Weatherford's suicide is unsuccessful—for which he is now relieved—and he rejoices that he has been able to aid his friend. The story is another in which Harben deals effectively with characters who are not mountaineers. Essentially a two-character sketch, it reads smoothly and naturally. Conventional as its plot summary seems, it also contains suspense and irony, with an O. Henry flavor.

"A Mountain Match-Maker" is a rural version of the Cinderella story. Cinderella is Mary Calhoun, a servant to the harsh Widow Trumley and her three plain, flighty daughters. The fairy godmother is Mr. Buford, an old boarder of Widow Trumley's, who arranges a match between Mary and the prince of the story,

Jasper Long, proprietor of the local grocery store. The story is
pointless, but charming and full of atmosphere. Mr. Buford's kind
meddling anticipates Harben's best-loved character, homespun
philosopher Abner Daniel, while Jasper Long is obviously
Harben himself during his own storekeeping days. His old habit
of avoiding customers is emphasized: "He made me go in the
back room so we could be undisturbed, an' while we was thar a
man come in the store an' begun to poke around like he wanted
to buy som'n'; but Long said, . . . 'Don't make any noise; he'll go
out in a minute,' an' so the man did. I reckon he thought
ever'body had gone to dinner."[23]

Another slight story, but one with realistic descriptions of rural
life, is "A Question of Valor" (Century, July, 1903). Young Albert
Lee is called a coward by his sweetheart, Carrie Turner, because
he remains neutral in her land dispute with his friend Jeff
Goodnow. But when Lee hears that Goodnow has been
slandering Carrie, he loads his gun and goes to face Goodnow at
the latter's grist mill. He finds Goodnow trapped between two
cog-wheels at the mill and saves his life, causing Goodnow to
relinquish his land claim fight with Carrie and to tell her of Lee's
courage and devotion to her. The lovers are reconciled and
married.

An indicator of Harben's growth as a writer is "A Filial
Pretence," a poignant story which could easily have been as
maudlin and sentimental as some of his earlier ones. Instead,
Harben uses restraint, with the result being an effective, moving
sketch. He curiously calls his hero "Albert Lee" and his heroine
"Carrie" again, even though the story was published the same
month as his other Albert Lee-Carrie story, "A Question of
Valor." This new Lee pretends to be the long-lost son of Mrs.
Meadow, whose real son—whom she never knew as an adult—
has just been hanged for murder. In the course of a short visit,
the old woman arranges a match between Lee and Carrie
Waters, younger daughter of the widow who runs the local
boarding house. Just before she is to leave, Mrs. Meadow dies
suddenly without discovering the deception: "At least, she didn't
find it out heer on earth, an' I believe when it's told her in
heaven it won't hurt."[24] The couple the old lady brought
together is left sad at her death, but happy that they have
discovered each other through her.

"Over the Mountain" is an ordinary story given extra flavor by the picturesque dialogue and realistic qualities which Harben imparts to his country characters. Overcome with futility, Gilbert Neal (also the name of the hero in Harben's 1908 novel, *Gilbert Neal*) leaves his home in the Cohutta Mountains after his sweetheart, Lucy Cobham, marries his rival, Abe Kineaster. Upon his return two years later, Neal learns that Kineaster had tricked Lucy into marrying him, that Kineaster has since deserted her—then died—and that Lucy is a destitute widow with a small baby. Neal and Lucy are married after he realizes that his prejudice against the child has melted: "Huh! I hain't once thought about its bein' his child. It's the livin' picture o' you, Lucy, an' that's all I kin think about when it's tucked up in my arms this a-way."[25]

Because Abner Daniel, Harben's most successful and best-loved literary creation (who appears in several novels), is the main character in "Two Birds with One Stone," the popularity of the story is assured. To prevent teenager Leon Waynright from making a romantic fool of himself with desperate old maid Sally Hawkes, Uncle Abner has Sim Leghorn, bachelor storekeeper, take her to the Sunday camp meeting. The plan not only breaks up Leon's infatuation with Sally, but it makes Sim's flippant sweetheart so jealous that she agrees to marry Sim. The story ends with meddlesome Uncle Abner planning to "pervide a husband o' some sort fer Sally Hawkes."[26]

"A Sprightly Heroine" consists entirely of Lizzie Wilson's trading and conversations with shy storekeeper Joe Larkin. Lizzie is a poor but proud young lady of the hills, who intends to marry a man she has been corresponding with but whom she has never seen. Larkin is desperately heartbroken at the news, for he has secretly loved Lizzie for years. When he discovers that Lizzie's fiancé never had any intentions of marrying her, Larkin finally proposes to her himself. She accepts: "Larkin's heart bounded. He was tingling from head to foot with the hot blood of new life. 'And in time,' he ventured, 'you may git so you love me a little.' 'Huh! what gal wouldn't?' she laughed, her eyes still avoiding his eager ones. 'I don't know but I do already— *some.* '"[27] The story is a delightful one, with two honest, real people as the main characters. Lizzie and Joe are Harben's models for the heroine and hero of *Dixie Hart* (1910); in fact, Harben used the plot of the story as a central incident in this novel.

"The Sale of the Mammoth Western" was also revised slightly and incorporated as several of the best chapters in *Dixie Hart*. Hiram Sedgewith, "the biggest crank in the country"[28] but a shrewd merchant, buys a rundown, bankrupt circus, the Mammoth Western, and sells everything—planks, ropes, tents, horses, wagons, pony, and cart—at a huge profit. Everything, that is, except the lion's cage, which nobody will buy. Finally George Mandel buys it from Sedgewith and profitably sells it to the local shoe repairman to be used as a new shop, so endearing himself to Sedgewith by his shrewd horsedealing that Sedgewith gives Mandel permission to marry his daughter Helen. Harben was wise to include this witty, warm story in his novel.

In "Circus Dan" (*Delineator*, March, 1910), Dan Pelham, a Yankee circus laborer, tires of his wandering life and decides to settle in Dayton, a small Georgia community. He is befriended by the elderly storekeeper, Hiram Throgmartin, who gives Dan a job in his store. Dan is an industrious worker, but because he is a Yankee—and a circus man as well—he is shunned by most of the community. His isolation is ended when he meets and marries Lucy Signer; for six months they are rapturously happy. Then Lucy and their unborn child die on the day the circus returns to Dayton. After her burial, a heartbroken Dan becomes resigned to a lonely life on the road as he rejoins the circus community. The story is overdone in parts, but it is moving; Pelham and Throgmartin are especially appealing, sensitive creations.

II Northern Georgia Sketches

The culmination of Harben's work with the short story came in 1900 with the publication of a collection of ten of the best which had previously appeared in various periodicals of the country. *Northern Georgia Sketches*, though now comparatively unknown, is "one of the better collections of regional American fiction."[29] This unassuming book of delightful stories about the homely lives of humble North Georgia mountaineers, white and black, is told with natural, skillful realism. The comments of Mary E. Wilkins are typical of the general reception of the collection: "They are thoroughly artistic and full of human interest. I did not know there was another southern writer . . . capable of writing such stories. They ought to be a great success."[30] The stories represent Harben at his best, and they brought him instant recognition as a local-color writer of real merit.

He had been hoping to bring out a collection of his stories for several years. When A. C. McClurg & Co. agreed to publish them, at the latter's suggestion he wrote his friend and mentor, Joel Chandler Harris, asking Harris to write a short introduction to the book: "I do hope you can see your way to the doing of this, for I am actually afraid McClurg will back out if I do not obey their wishes in the matter, although they highly appreciate the stories they have selected. I think their judgment in the selection is good and am sure that this book will give me a standing that nothing I have written could do. I have been urged to bring out this book by the best literary men in the country and am anxious to see it out."[31] Harris did not write the introduction, but the McClurg people did not back out, and Harben dedicated the book to Harris "in grateful acknowledgment of the kindly encouragement which made this book possible."[32]

The first story, "A Humble Abolitionist," apparently had as its origin Harben's father's predicament when he had been forced to take a slave as payment for a financial debt. Peter Gill and his wife Lucretia, a plain, religious couple who are completely opposed to slavery, are miserable at the prospect of finding themselves in the possession of Big Joe. With an air of tragic humor, Mrs. Gill moans, "The Lord only knows what we'll do. We are purty-lookin' folks to own a high-priced, stuck-up quality nigger" (15). The couple prepare for Big Joe as if he were a guest, giving him a room with a more comfortable bed than their own, a carpet, washstand, mirror, and pictures on the wall. Joe arrives and refuses to eat, stating that he intends to starve, and the Gills believe he thinks himself superior to them. Within a day the Gills' neighbors label them one-nigger, log-cabin aristocracy too superior to associate with the "poor white trash of the community." Finally Joe admits his trouble: in the business deal, he has been separated from Liza, his "yaller gal" who had been freed by her new owners. "Then it wasn't because you thought yorese'f so much better'n me'n my wife that you wanted to dump yorese'f into eternity?" (40-41). The obvious, simple solution to the problems of both the Gills and Joe is to free Joe. This is done. Joe and Liza are married, and the Gills, once again on equal footing with their neighbors, admit that they "wouldn't pass another day like yistiddy fer all the slaves in Georgia" (44).

The New York *Times* review of *Northern Georgia Sketches* was especially appreciative of "A Humble Abolitionist," and noted that "this tale of a very black 'white elephant' . . . might well have been expanded into a more elaborate study."[33] The story is typical of Harben's attitude toward the black, for the plight of the Gills is essentially the plight of Harben. Opposed to slavery, they are yet caught in the middle of the system. They want to seat Joe at their dinner table, but cannot bring themselves to do so because it is not done, because "it ain't common fer folks to eat with their slaves" (31). The Gills show far more compassion and decency than their neighbors, the Duncans, who laugh at the Gills' predicament and sneer, "A nigger ain't like no other livin' cre'ture" (22).

The conclusion of "A Humble Abolitionist" is rather uninspiring, but in "The Whipping of Uncle Henry" the resolution is thoroughly logical and strong, not at all innocuous. Jasper Pelham, a compassionate slaveowner, is called back to his home in Georgia from North Carolina to whip Uncle Henry, a slave who refuses to obey the ill-bred overseer Cobb in his master's absence. Taking two long hickory whips and Uncle Henry to the woods for the necessary punishment, the pious Pelham has Uncle Henry kneel with him in prayer to make the beating "righteous." "Lord, on this occasion it seems my duty to punish him for disobedience, an' we pray Thee to sanction what is about to take place with Thy grace" (65). To Pelham's surprise, the bold slave continues the prayer on his own:

Thou knowest that I am Thy humble servant. . . . Thou knowest that I have for a long time harbored the belief that the black man has some rights that he don't git under existin' laws, but which, Thy will be done, will come in due time, like the harvest follows the plantin'. Thou knowest, an' I know, that Henry Pelham is nigher to Thee than a dumb brute, an' that it ain't no way to lift a nigger up to beat 'im like a horse or a ox. I have said this to Thee in secret prayer, time an' ag'in, an' Thou knowest that before Thee I have vowed that I would die before any man, white or black, kin beat the blood out'n my back. I may have brought trouble and vexation to Marse Jasper, I don't dispute that, but he had no business puttin' me under that low-down-white-trash overseer an' goin' off so far. Heavenly Father, thou knowest I love Marse Jasper, an' I would work fer 'im till I die; but he is ready to put the lash to me an' disgrace me before my wife an' children. Give my arms strength, Lord, to defend myself even against him—against him who has, up to now, won my respect an' love by forbearance an' kindness. He has said it, Lord—he has said that he will whip me; but I've said, also, that no man shall do it. Give me strength to battle fer the right, an' if he is hurt—bad hurt—may the Lord have mercy on him! This I ask through the mercy an' the blood of the Lord Jesus Christ. Amen. (67-69)

As a result of this defiance, Pelham spares Henry the whipping, since the prayer makes him both fear and respect the black man. The pair, united once more, make an agreement to keep their actions (or nonactions) a secret, and Pelham gives Henry the responsibility of maintaining a certain tract of land with no supervision from Cobb. "The plan suited Cobb exactly; but when Mr. Pelham came home the following summer it was hard to hear him say that Uncle Henry had accomplished more than any three of the other negroes" (74).

Uncle Henry's prayer is a powerful statement of black feelings and dissatisfactions before the Emancipation; its message is clear and modern. It shows that however condescending Harben might have been in some of his previous works, he was nevertheless moving toward a point at which he could boldly state the unjust predicament of the black man. Certainly one of Harben's best, the story was selected by Richard Beale Davis, C. Hugh Holman, and Louis D. Rubin, Jr., for inclusion in their recent anthology, *Southern Writing, 1585-1920.*

"A Filial Impulse," the story Harben's fellow editors at the *Youth's Companion* had recommended to the *Century,* has charm and pathos. Jim Bradley, a middleage bachelor who runs a general store in the West, learns that his brother was killed two years before and that his mother is in need of help. Since Bradley still feels guilty for having after continuous arguments deserted them ten years earlier, he sells his store and stock and returns to Georgia. Finding his feeble mother overjoyed to see him, he makes plans to buy a plantation and make her last days happy ones. The story achieves its charm from the colloquialisms and the realistic dialogue—especially between Bradley and the men in his store—and between Bradley and his mother when they meet again. This long recognition scene has a low-keyed tone which adds to its effectiveness: its slow pace conveys the old woman's gradual recognition of her son and her realization that she need no longer be a servant to the family with which she has been forced to stay.

Though "A Filial Impulse" contains no black characters, the

fourth story, "The Sale of Uncle Rastus," is almost wholly
concerned with slaves. Uncle Rastus, Herbert Putnam's favorite
slave, has been ill and will never be able to work again. His illness
fills Uncle Rastus with dismay, for Putnam is being forced by his
brother, Colonel George Putnam, to sell his plantation and
slaves, and "Unc' Rastus, de mos' valuables' one, tuk sick, en now
Aunt Milly an' de chillun won't fetch ernough ter do much good"
(116). In desperate determination to help his beloved master,
Uncle Rastus awes the spectators at the auction block by a
grueling display of strength. The greedy brother bids highly to
buy Uncle Rastus, but Putnam, though a lifelong enemy, tells him
the truth, not wanting to see him cheated. The two brothers are
reconciled on the spot, and George allows Herbert to keep his
plantation and his worshipful slaves.

The second half of the tale, melodramatic and full of false
pathos, is redeemed by the first half through Harben's conception and treatment of black life. Aunt Milly, Uncle Rastus's
wife, supervises a neighborhood possum feast. Harben's handling
of the affair is believable and lifelike throughout. "Nelse got out
his bones and began to play, and Len and Caesar danced jogs till
they sank to the floor in exhaustion. After this, plantation songs
were sung, ghost-stories were told, and it was late when they
went back to their homes" (119-20). Because Harben tells of
these activities with obvious affection and understanding, the
blacks are depicted not as the primitive animals some of the
whites in the story consider them to be, but as feeling, reasonable
human beings. Uncle Rastus, though a different kind of man from
Uncle Henry, wholly subservient to his master, attains heroic
status through his actions nonetheless.

"The Convict's Return," about a horsethief's homecoming and
his attempts to win back his divorced wife, is another simple but
moving sketch. Dick Wakeman's sister-in-law, immediately
sympathetic with him, tries to help him gain reconciliation with
her sister Marty. Dick takes over the duties on the farm, but his
exwife refuses to acknowledge his presence. Finally, after he
runs off her suitor, "the most triflin' fop in the county" (137),
Marty relents and admits Dick to her heart and home again. The
story contains some concrete, knowledgeable descriptions of a
small farm and the duties necessary to keep it going—a hog
killing, for example, and such details as "a fire's no fire without a
backlog" (147). Harben hits the precise note of the characters'

embarrassment and awkwardness in a scene in which Dick forgets to say grace at the dinner table: "A body that's tuk his meals on a tin plate in a row o' fellers waitin' fer the'r turn four years hand-runnin', ain't expected to—" (149).

A completely captivating story is "A Rural Visitor." Lucinda Gibbs, a mountain widow, is determined to visit her son and his wife in New York City; her storekeeper neighbor, widower Joel Lowry, decides to accompany her and transact some business during his week's stay. On the train the naive, lonely pair become quite close; but they part at the railroad station in the city. When Joel calls on Lucinda a week later to tell her he is going back to Georgia, she yearns to return herself: "I don't dare to say a word, fer Amos seems tickled to death over all that Sally gits up; but, Joel, I'm mighty nigh dead. Like a born idiot, I told 'em in my last letter that I'd stay three months, an' now, as the Lord is my help an' stay, I don't believe I can make out another week" (187). Two weeks later, in Georgia, Joel hears that Lucinda has returned. When he visits her, they decide to get married. "Well, you see, the—the notion seemed to strike both of us when we was travelin' together, an'—an' she admitted that she was a leetle grain afeered that ef we didn't see one another ag'in fer three months that the notion might wear off. Railly, she's tickled to death, fur now she says she kin give Amos an' Sally a sensible reason fer wantin' to get back home" (195).

The understated story is charmingly humorous throughout. Lucinda and Joel are among the most thoroughly likable mountaineers in Harben's galaxy of characters. Both are iron-willed individuals who must finally reveal their emotions. Their awkward courtship is treated with engaging warmth and understanding. Harben always was better at realistically portraying older mountain people than younger ones, for they are more set in their ways, more natural, less conscious of pretentiousness; Lucinda and Joel are perfect illustrations of these characteristics. The opening description of Lucinda, a typical "cracker" woman, is especially good: "Lucinda Gibbs stood in the corner of the rail fence behind her cottage. Her face was damp with perspiration, and her heavy iron-gray hair had become disarranged and hung down her back below the skirt of her gingham sun-bonnet. She was raking the decayed leaves and dead weeds into her tender strawberry sprouts and mentally calculating on the abundant crop of the luscious fruit later in the spring" (167).

Pole Baker, one of Harben's most famous recurring characters, is foreshadowed in Jim Trundle, a "lazy, worthless vagabond" as he himself finally admits. "Jim Trundle's Crisis" begins when Trundle receives a letter from the Regulators, a self-appointed vigilante team formed for the protection of their mountain settlement. The letter reads, in part:

You are no earthly account, an no amount of talkin seems to do you any good. Yore childern are in tatters an without food, an you jest wont do nothin fer them. This might hav gone on longer without our action, but last Wednesday you let yore sick wife go to the field in the hot brilin sun, and she was seed by a responsible citizen in a faintin condition, while you was on the creek banks a fishin in the shade.

To night exactly at eight oclock we are comin after you in full force to give you a sound lickin. Yore wife and childern would be better off without you, and we advise you to leave the country before that time. If we find you at home at eight oclock you may count on a sore back. (204)

A deeper insight into Trundle's character reveals that he has genuine love and tenderness in his soul. "Nature had, indeed, made him happy in rags, oblivious to material things. Had he been endowed with education he might have become a poet. He saw strange, transcendent possibilities in the blue skies; in the green growing things; in the dun heights of the mountains. . . . If only those men really understood him they would pardon his shortcomings. No human being could knowingly lash a man feeling as he felt" (206-07). Trundle awakens to a realization of his own better nature and decides to take his punishment from the Regulators. He meets them away from his house to save his wife and children the embarrassment of the "lickin'." After the men see that he has genuinely repented, they decide that to beat him would serve no purpose. A new man, Trundle makes his way back to his waiting, still devoted wife.

"The Courage of Ericson," a tightly knit story of the Civil War, involves Confederate Private John Ericson, who is wounded in a skirmish in his home community. He takes refuge at the house of his estranged sweetheart, Sally Tripp, whose family fights for the Union. "She 'lowed ef I jined the Confederacy I needn't ever look her way any more. Her father an' only brother went to the Union side, an' she blamed me fer wantin' to go with my folks" (230). Sally refuses to aid him until she sees that he is wounded. The Union soldiers are searching every house in the territory for hidden Rebels, and while Ericson is unconscious, Sally and her grandfather dress him in her dead brother's Union uniform and deceive the search party. When Ericson sees that Sally still loves him, their future together after the war ends is assured. The story, which more appropriately might have been called "The Courage of Sally Tripp," is told in a terse manner. The action moves quickly, and Harben handles all characters and situations believably, especially his dramatization of the division of sympathies in North Georgia during the Civil War.

One of the best stories in the collection is "The Heresy of Abner Calihan." One critic stated that it is a good example of what the local-color story should have been but usually was not: "There is no quaintness in the rustic characters, no prettiness in their way of life, almost no romantic appeal at all."[34] The situation is one Harben frequently would emphasize in the series of novels he would later write: "an individual with strength of character who opposes the will of the community."[35] Abner Calihan, a member of the church and a good, industrious citizen, is to be tried for heresy by the elders of his church for speaking out against the fundamentalist belief in salvation by faith rather than works, for doubting the existence of a fire and brimstone hell, and for refusing to take the Bible literally. "We jest *had* to take action. . . . The opinions you have expressed . . . are so undoctrinal an' so p'int blank ag'in' the articles of faith that, believin' as you seem to believe, you are plumb out o' j'int with Big Cabin Church, an' a resky man in any God-feerin' community" (271). The elders go to Abner's house and confront him with the issue in front of his wife and daughter, who are "quivering with soundless sobs. They had forsaken him. He was an alien in his own house, a criminal convicted beneath his own roof" (272). He finally gives in, not in defeat, but simply to save his wife and daughter from the public disgrace that would follow his expulsion if he resisted: "I am ag'in' bringin' reproach on my wife an' child. . . . You all know best. I reckon I have been too forward an' too eager to heer myself talk. . . . Ef it's jest the same to you'uns you may let the charge drap, an'—an' in future I'll give no cause fer complaint" (275). Thus, Abner shrewdly holds on to his ideals and his questioning nature, even though he is forced to compromise for practical reasons. The story goes beyond local matters to a universal problem: the individual's right to think and speak in a community as he feels he must.[36]

It is a pithy, direct story to which Harben loans some authentic descriptions of the environs of an average Southern farmer. Abner's home is a weatherboarded, unpainted log cabin surrounded by an orchard, with its stained cider press, a chip-strewn yard full of cords of wood, a log barn with a stable-yard, and a green meadow interrupted by cornfields and a creek. The combination country store-post office, the meeting place for everyone within ten miles of the spot, is filled with disorderly displays of everything "from shoe-eyes to sacks of guano" (256). The sight is "enough to make an orderly housewife shudder with horror" (256). Abner himself, obviously a mountaineer extension of Stanley Clayton in *Almost Persuaded* and a foreshadowing of Abner Daniel in Harben's later novels, is graphically described: "His blue jean trousers were carelessly stuck into the tops of his clay-stained boots, and he wore a sack-coat, a 'hickory' shirt, and a leather belt. . . . He threw his tobacco-quid away, noisily washed out his mouth, and took a long drink from the gourd dipper" (257-58).

The last story in the collection, "The Tender Link," is another sketch of filial love and obligations. Lucian Laramore, a promising young writer who left his home in Georgia because he disliked his stepfather, returns when he learns his mother is ill. When he sees the squalid living conditions of her house, he uses the ten thousand dollars he has saved to buy a comfortable plantation for her and his half-sisters and brother. He returns to New York after reconciling himself with his stepfather and being assured that his mother will be well and happy in her new home. The story is sentimental but realistic, and the reunion scene between mother and son, a masterpiece of understatement. It shows the absence of expression of sentiment among relatives of the poorer classes in the hill country. "He took one of her hard, thin hands and bent over her. Should he kiss her? She had not taught him to do so when he was a child, and he had never kissed her in his life, but he had seen the world and grown wiser. He turned her face toward him and pressed his lips to her. She was much surprised, and drew herself from him and wiped her mouth with a corner of the sheet, but he knew she was pleased" (288-89). The scene was so successful that Harben used it again, almost verbatim, as the nucleus of the subplot in *Ann Boyd*.

William Dean Howells, the most influential literary man of the day, called *Northern Georgia Sketches* "one of the best and truest books I have read for many a day."[37] So impressed was Howells with the collection that he wrote Harben asking if the author would not submit to Harper and Brothers for Harper's "American Novel Series" the manuscript of a novel also set in North Georgia.[38] Harben eagerly complied. He had found himself. The great majority of his remaining twenty-three novels, in fact, were set in Georgia. Thus he clearly followed Howells's advice to "stick to your own soil." Though he still did an occasional short story, his primary interest for the rest of his life became the writing of regional novels concerning his home country and people.

CHAPTER 4

Critical Recognition: 1901-1910

THE first decade of the twentieth century comprised Harben's finest years in all areas. His novels about North Georgia met with critical approval by the literati; he was recognized as an authentic delineator of the backwoods people he knew so well. His popularity among readers continued to impress his publishers and to flatter Harben himself. His social graces and charm made him widely accepted in the literary circles of New York, and he and his wife Maybelle became well-known society figures of the city.

I Life in the City

After settling near Columbia University, the Harbens plunged into New York's social life, Maybelle with some apprehension since she considered herself a simple country girl. They became intimate with some of the literary giants of the period, among them Ella Wheeler Wilcox, one of their first callers; Booth Tarkington; Ellen Glasgow, to whose work Harben's has been compared; the Hamlin Garlands, who lived nearby and were quite close to the Harbens ("Mrs. Garland was a great believer in fresh air and used to put her baby in a basket on the fire escape, much to my husband's discomfort."[1]); Edwin Markham, "a grand old patriarch"[2]; Edith Wharton; the Theodore Dreisers, whom they often visited; and Albert Bigelow Paine, through whom they met Samuel L. Clemens. Maybelle poured tea at a reception given by the Paines for Clemens, who "seemed tired and asked if he might sit beside me for a while. He asked if I would tell him something about the Southern Negroes, their songs and superstitions. I think once again that my Southern accent was a center of interest — it must have been very noticeable."[3] Later, the Harbens attended a tea at Clemens's home: "I shall always

78

remember the great humorist, his white hair a halo around his head, laughing heartily at a joke my husband was telling."[4] Of course, William Dean Howells, Harben's new literary godfather, remained a close friend to the couple; "Mr. Howells did many kind things for my husband."[5]

Maybelle's account of a formal dinner reflects her innocence and charm as she sat in her homemade yellow chiffon dress opposite Mrs. Cornelius Vanderbilt, "who ate with long white gloves on!"[6] One wealthy guest told Maybelle that she should have her portrait painted in the dress; "little he knew we could hardly pay the rent."[7] But after constant socializing with the literary world at dinners, receptions, and operas, Maybelle soon became as elegant and sophisticated as anyone, and her husband was extremely proud of his young wife.

The Harbens were by no means wealthy, at least in the early years of their marriage. An indication of their financial condition was their being forced to decline a presentation at court to King Edward VII, an arrangement made through Harben's British relatives. "We counted our dollars over and over, but they would not stretch for the trip. My husband received a great deal of free advertising, however, and I was asked many times for photographs, which were printed all over the country."[8]

Even away from the South, Harben had two experiences with blacks which left memorable impressions. He learned a lesson in Northern customs when he called his black janitor's wife "Auntie," thinking he was being polite since it was a Southern custom to refer to older black women in this way. She resented his familiarity and answered, "I am no kin of yours. Please call me Mrs. Williams when you speak to me hereafter!"[9] The other association was more pleasant. The Harbens had a black cook who became a fast friend, and who was a help to Harben in his writings about the blacks. This cook took pride in his work, and he later dedicated one of his novels to her in appreciation of her aid. After his death she kept a watchful eye on Maybelle, visiting her often.[10]

The Harbens had three children: William Chandler, born in 1899; Eric Marion, born in 1903; and Elizabeth, born in 1913. On the birth of their first child, Robert Loveman wrote a poem for them entitled "The Harben Boy."[11] The second son, Eric, died at the age of eight; Maybelle was so despondent that Harben had her niece stay with them in New York for several months to occupy her time.[12] Harben himself was deeply grieved ("It has completely upset my nerves—and heart")[13] but the final effect on him was a fascination with immortality. His wife reported that he became a man "whose chief desire was a solution of the hereafter. He read hundreds of books on the subject and tried to get all with whom he came in contact to give him their views. He died feeling that only by death could he solve his soul's desires; he went into the beyond with a feeling of a great adventure."[14] He did not allow the thought to cloud his family's happiness, but there was always "a wistful look in his eyes as if searching into the infinite for the face that had gone ahead."[15] This interest is particularly evident in his posthumously published work, *The Divine Event.*

During this decade Harben developed some theories and methods of writing that he adhered to for the rest of his career. Always a prolific writer, he claimed that he did not allow demands on him to lure him into hasty, careless productions. He was forced to decline many social invitations once he became involved in a new novel. In a letter to the daughter of his friend Frank Stanton, he explained his views thusly:

I am awfully sorry that I can't come Tuesday evg. The truth is that I am simply *crazy*. After 6 months idle worry over my next book I am at last at work on the first writing & I can not put it down night or day. You know something of the moods of literary men having a genuine poet at home, but even poets who write short things don't hold a torch to a novelist whose duty for a whole year hangs on *one* piece of work. . . . Poverty knocks at the door of the writer who fails to work. When the moment comes, you know I told you that at such a time I must not be interested in a thing outside of my plot & characters & so social amusements have to be avoided. . . . I shall lead the life of a Harlem hermit till about Feb. 15. Now, *do* forgive my lack of hospitality. I am only another literary crank, who is not half as useful to normal women as men in other walks of life.[16]

He composed on a typewriter, never by longhand, and he would not begin a story until he knew how it would end, until he had a rough draft of it in his mind. On a stroll in Morningside Park one day in 1905, he was accused by a reporter of being as idle as any of the other walkers there. He laughed and brought out several sheets from a tiny scratch pad, showing the reporter the notes for the first eleven chapters of a new novel. "I jotted them down this morning, but I have been planning those chapters and thinking about them for the last four months. Now I have them all before me—in my mind, you understand—and I can put them down on paper without more ado. And the rest of it will come easily; because I have thought it all out. . . . When I come to put it on paper I shall be familiar with every detail of it."[17] The "putting on paper" of a novel took him no longer than three months, but he often spent six to eight months previous to that in planning his story and working out its problems. "It might look as if I was idling, but I give all my thoughts to the story, and I don't have time to do anything else. I think about my story, and nothing else."[18] His method worked for him, for he averaged a novel a year for the rest of his life.

II   The Woman Who Trusted

The first novel Harben published after *Northern Georgia Sketches* was *The Woman Who Trusted: A Story of Literary Life in New York* (1901), a manuscript that the Henry Altemis Company had already purchased before Harper and Brothers began their long association with Harben. Though the novel more appropriately fits its subtitle, Harben understood the value of a more romantic idea to the reading public, so it became *The Woman Who Trusted*. Despite the unfortunate title, the novel is an honest analysis of the politics of the literary world of New York City at the turn of the century. Sometimes romantic, sometimes hard, it always rings true.

The Harben hero here is Wilmot Burian, a fledgling writer from a small town in Georgia who gives up his beginning law practice to enter the literary world of New York. He leaves behind Muriel Fairchild, who has given him her full encouragement concerning his literary desires. Upon arriving in New York, Burian discovers that the publishing firm which had accepted his novel has gone bankrupt; yet he cannot legally recover his manuscript until a new friend, Mrs. Sennett, a rich widow in her fifties, intervenes with her money and charm and gives it to a more reputable firm. In an impulsive show of gratitude, Burian proposes marriage to her, unaware that she is notorious in her "silly craze for Fauntleroy lovers."[19] This proposal is witnessed by the spiteful Mrs. Dolly Langdon, a New York gossip columnist who wastes no time in exploiting the matter in her column, ridiculing the engaged pair.

Meanwhile, Muriel, who arrives in New York with her voice

teacher, completely understands his predicament, and stands by Burian. She talks with Mrs. Langdon, who, in a burst of guilt followed by good will, succeeds in persuading Mrs. Sennett to give up the young writer. In her next column, Mrs. Langdon rights the wrong her venomous pen has done. Burian's novel is published; he takes a job in London as correspondent for a newspaper, and is eventually joined by Muriel and their newly married friends, Louis and Aline Chester, whose love affair forms a subplot to the story.

The story of Wilmot Burian is, in part at least, the story of Will N. Harben's early literary career, for the similarities in their lives are obvious. Burian's lack of interest in law practice corresponds to Harben's lack of interest in a business career. Both begin by writing short stories and finally a novel. Both are objects of ridicule by some of their fellow Georgians because of the realistic dialects they use: "Who wants to know anything about these mountain people and their wretched dialect that we have heard all our lives?" (96). They are about the same age when they undertake their literary careers; they are both dashing, handsome young men who are popular in the literary salons of New York City, especially with the aristocratic ladies of the period. A society columnist, possibly the model for Dolly Langdon, described Harben as "a tall, dark-eyed man with a soft voice and somewhat nervous manner. He is fast becoming a familiar figure at many of the literary salons and Bohemian gatherings of the town. . . . Mr. Harben has located in New York and, with a well-known woman writer as sponsor, has received much local attention."[20] Insofar as other columns linked him, though not necessarily romantically, with a writer-turned-literary-sponsor, Mary E. Bryan, the similarity between Harben and Mrs. Bryan and Burian and Mrs. Sennett is apparent.

Muriel Fairchild has many characteristics of Maybelle Chandler, Harben's wife. Both are approximately the same age; both are vital, trusting young women who encourage their respective sweethearts; and both achieve limited fame for their singing voices. Whereas Harben was more than twenty years older than Maybelle, Burian is only ten years older than Muriel; but even this fact is reconciled by the subplot involving Louis Chester, a man of forty, who loves and eventually marries Aline Weyland, an eighteen-year-old girl. Thus Harben entwined his own life with the lives of both Burian and Chester.

The Woman Who Trusted is not one of Harben's best stories, but it does provide an accurate picture of literary life in New York, as well as some insights into Harben's own struggles there ten years before.

III   Westerfelt

When William Dean Howells asked Harben on behalf of Harper and Brothers to submit a novel in the same vein as *Northern Georgia Sketches,* Harben sent *Westerfelt,* which had previously been rejected by all the leading publishers in the country, including Harper. This time it was immediately accepted. Its publication in 1901 marked the beginning of a permanent relationship between Harben and Harper; the firm published all twenty-two novels Harben wrote from then on. The book was given a special promotion as a part of Harper's new "American Novel Series," and a separate page in the novel announces: "*Westerfelt* is the sixth of twelve American novels to be published by Harper & Brothers during 1901, written for the most part by new American writers, and dealing with different phases of contemporary American life."[21]

Harben had called his book *The Remorse of John Westerfelt* originally, but wisely shortened the title.[22] John Westerfelt, the guilt ridden hero, a rich young man of Darley, had been courting Sally Dawson, without ever seriously considering marrying her. When Sally drowns herself because of this rejected love, her mother, Sue Dawson, a widow almost insane in her grief, relentlessly dogs Westerfelt with poison-pen letters and vicious accusations. Full of remorse and badly shaken, he finally leaves Darley to manage a stable he has bought in a town several hundred miles away, where he meets Harriet Floyd, daughter of the local hotel owner. After she nurses him back to health when he is stabbed in a fight with the town bully, Toot Wambush, Harriet and Westerfelt fall in love. Due to a misunderstanding, however, Westerfelt believes Harriet loves Toot, and cannot bring himself to admit his love to the apparently "soiled" girl. Mrs. Dawson, who has traced him to his new town, resumes her accusations before finally, aided by the wisdom of Martha Bradley, a friend of both Mrs. Dawson and Westerfelt, becoming a righteous, changed woman at a revival meeting. The misunderstanding between Westerfelt and Harriet is worked out, and the young couple face a future of happiness together.

Except for the last part of the book, when Harben gets bogged down in too much romantic nonsense, *Westerfelt* is an exciting story that moves rapidly. The fight between Westerfelt and Toot Wambush is a realistic and dramatic scene. The customs of the hills are authentically described — such events as quilting parties, hog killings, and square dances — and the dialogue and wisdom of the mountaineers ring natural and true. The usual local-color tendency to manufacture nostalgia for the past or to inspire tenderness for peculiarities of a region is missing. Like Ellen Glasgow, Harben offers his readers the common man, unadorned by frills and excesses. For example, a realistic touch is demonstrated when the matter-of-fact uncle of Sally, Peter Slogan, discusses a coffin for his dead niece: "I've got the exact length o' the body. I 'lowed that would be the best way. I reckon they kin tell me at the store how much play a corpse ort to have at each end. I've noticed that coffins always look longer, a sight, than the pusson ever did that was to occupy 'em, but I thought ef I tuck the exact measure —" (24-25). Such deft statements immediately label the character who speaks them as a coarse, crude mountaineer who does not mean to be vulgar and unmoved, but who feels the necessity to be blunt and honest about the necessary arrangements. Harben is excellent at characterizing his people in such a way. He lets their actions and dialogue label them, thereby avoiding laboriously long descriptive passages.

An early version of the Ku Klux Klan is found in the novel in the form of the White Caps, a dreaded vigilante committee that "takes care of their own" in their territory. The White Caps forcibly take Westerfelt because they think he has informed the sheriff of their moonshining activities. The lynch scene that follows is melodramatic, improbable, but exciting as Westerfelt faces the mob and convinces them that he is innocent. In fact, the mob turns on Toot Wambush instead and runs him out of town, threatening to tar and feather him if he objects. The Harben hero always has a power of rhetoric sufficient to completely turn the tables on an unruly, vicious mob until the members reach the point that they actually cheer the very person they have intended to lynch.

Other familiar characteristics of later Harben novels appear in *Westerfelt*. A happy ending for the decent characters and deserved punishment for the evil ones became a common Harben device, as did the misunderstanding between hero and heroine. But this novel is more poetic and mellow in its description of physical details than later ones, such as in the scene in which Sally Dawson, a sensitively etched character, overhears her talkative aunt gossip about Westerfelt's interest in another girl: "A look of wretched conviction stamped itself on the girl's delicate features. Slowly she turned to pick up her flowers, and went with them to the mantel-piece. There was an empty vase half filled with water, and into it she tried to place the stems, but they seemed hard to manage in her quivering fingers, and she finally took the flowers to her own room across the passage. They heard the sagging door scrape the floor as she closed it after her" (7-8). Or the rendering of Sally's funeral procession, seen from his estate by Westerfelt, who cannot attend the ceremony because of the accusations of Sally's mother:

Westerfelt's eyes were glued to the one-horse wagon at the gate, for it contained the coffin, and was moving like a thing alive. Behind it walked six men, swinging their hats in their hands. Next followed Slogan's rickety buggy with its threatening wheels, driven by Peter. The bent figure of the widow in black sat beside him. Other vehicles fell in behind, and men, women, and children on foot, carrying wild flowers, dogwood blossoms, pink and white honeysuckle, and bunches of violets, brought up the rear. (32-33)

With such understated descriptions, Harben showed signs of becoming a first-rate writer. Unfortunately, such scenes were scarce in many of his later novels.

The female characters in *Westerfelt* are particularly interesting. Harriet Floyd is typical of Harben's young heroines— beautiful, intelligent, brave, and completely honest. Harben was sometimes criticized for the sugary formality of his young females, although they are no more stilted than some of the heroines of his contemporary writers, including William Dean Howells, Theodore Dreiser, and Henry James. Harben's heroines are open and honest with themselves; there is not as much artificiality in them as in some of the women characters of his contemporaries.

But it is in the older women that Harben excelled—and he created vivid portrayals of three such women in this novel. Sue Dawson, Sally's mother, is a true friend to her daughter before Sally dies. Her transformation into a vindictive, hate filled

woman bent on vengeance is made reasonable and understandable by Harben. She is a dangerous woman, yet also pathetic and
pitiable. Her religious conversion at the camp meeting, though
overly sudden and coincidental, Harben makes plausible because
he understates Mrs. Dawson's actions and words. She retains her
proud individuality even as she forgives Westerfelt and returns
to her sister. This sister, Clarissa Slogan, is another outstanding
minor character. She is a busybody who is always right and who
at the beginning of the book seems as she nags Sally to have no
feelings for her niece's predicament. But the reader soon realizes
that she means no harm, and that her brusqueness is merely a
device used to hide her sensitivity and inability to express her
true feelings.

Finally, the most delightful, realistic woman character in the
novel is Martha Bradley, with whom Westerfelt stays for a time.
Martha is a backwoods matron who has plenty of the *joie de
vivre* and constantly shows it. Though she likes to meddle in
Westerfelt's life, it is always because she wants to help him—
which she always succeeds in doing. She is a great tease,
especially with her husband Luke: "He seed me a-takin' on with
Mis' Dawson, an' he thinks I've got a fresh dose o' religion. I
didn't let 'im know no better, an' he was grum all the way home.
He can't put up with a Christian of the excitable sort. Hush, don't
say a word; watch me devil him, but ef you don't keep a straight
face I'll bust out laughin'. Lordy, I feel good somehow" (282). So
does the reader, for it is in such character portrayals as these that
Harben manages to infuse fresh vitality into what could have
easily been stereotypical mountain matrons. His first-hand
knowledge of such women is apparent in his honest depiction of
them.

In his "Editor's Easy Chair" column, Howells praised *Westerfelt* for its "simplicity of a high and fine sort," for its "potent
imagination with the play of human passions in an original
rearrangement of the world-old drama," and for Harben's
courage in presenting fiction with common people and not lords
and knights.[23] Nine years later Howells continued his praise of
the novel:

If Mr. Harben . . . could have sustained his story of "Westerfelt" on the
level of its opening chapters, he would have created a masterpiece
worthy of the great modern Spaniards or Russians, and rare in our

besotted Anglo-Saxon fiction, where it is supposed that the actions and
not the emotions are the drama. At times throughout he does return to
that level, and the tale is always simply faithful to the unsophisticated
circumstance of its people; but it is not so constant to it as to merit the
praise I should like to give. I could not praise it too much for the
strength and courage with which it portrays the anguish of the poor girl
who drowns herself, and the bitter hate of the mother for the man who
had forgotten rather than slighted her. Afterwards there is something
fine in the way the mother's rancor loses itself in her better knowledge
of the facts, and the story is bravely true to life in its course away from
the tragic beginning to the fortunate ending; a weaker hand might have
left it steeped in gloom.[24]

With such praise from the dean of American Letters, Harben's
first important regional novel may be considered a success.

IV   Abner Daniel

Abner Daniel, Harben's most popular book, was published in
1902. Even the severest critics found in it more virtues than
faults. One complimented Harben on his "admirable unob-
trusiveness,"[25] another called the novel "a very pleasant and
restful book."[26] The main plot—"this everlasting business about
an investment and a mortgage"[27]—concerns young Alan Bishop's
efforts to recover a large amount of money that his father, a land
speculator in North Carolina (like Harben's father), has lost in
buying worthless tracts of timber land. With the help of a lawyer
friend, Rayburn Miller; his uncle, Abner Daniel; and his
desperado friend, Pole Baker, he succeeds after many setbacks.
In the process he wins the love of Dolly Barclay, a spirited young
socialite of Darley who is "all wool an' a yard wide," according to
Uncle Abner.[28] A subplot involves Miller's change from a man
who is cynical about love into one who is enraptured by it when
he becomes enamored of Alan's sister Adele. The story is fast-
moving and interesting in itself, but its main purpose is to furnish
a setting for the exploits and anecdotes of Abner Daniel and Pole
Baker.

Abner, who gives his name to the book, is actually a minor
figure who holds the threads of the story together. Self-reliant,
unaffected by society's demands for conformity, and always
ready to unselfishly aid those who need help, he is the bachelor
uncle of the Bishop family. He has "a natural tendency to turn

everything into a jest—even the serious things of life" (8) and is
full of homespun Georgia philosophy. The Southern counterpart
of David Harum (though some critics argued that Abner was
vastly superior to David), Uncle Abner and his dry humor and
philosophy were quoted all over America. "The wust things I
ever seed was sometimes at the root o' the best. Manure is a bad
thing, but a cake of it will produce a daisy bigger 'n any in the
field" (81). Or "Old women an' old bachelors . . . are alike. The
longer a man lives without a woman the more he gits like one. I
reckon that's beca'se the man 'at lives with one don't see nothin'
wuth copyin' in 'er, an' vice-a-versy" (20). Like Huck Finn,
Abner compares men to hogs which have been rooting up fresh
crops: "Ef they'd a-rooted in straight rows an' not gone too nigh
the stalks they mought 'a' done the crap more good than harm,
but the'r aim or intention, one or t'other, was bad. Folks is that
way; mighty few of 'em root—when they root at all—fer
anybody but the'rselves" (8).

A more serious side of Abner Daniel is inherent in Harben's
conception of the man:

I was once attracted to a little cautious group of mountain freethinkers
and budding philosophers. They were waking up to the conviction that
the old creeds and dogmas did not reach to the limits of their
conception of what divine revelation ought to be. They still remained
members of churches, because no respectable men in the mountains
could be otherwise, but they ceased to pray in public, deserted their
Bible classes which they used to instruct, and seldom took the
sacrament of the Lord's Supper. They were more interesting to me than
all the rest put together because, with furtive glances here and there,
they were actually *sneaking* out of darkness into light. One of their
leaders, whom I afterward named "Abner Daniel," was an oratorical
genius. He not only prayed but spoke in meeting, and his words formed
such a subtle subterfuge and skilful balancing on the fence of opinion
that he inspired both the bound and the unbound.[29]

Abner, who "ain't none of yore shoutin' kind of Christians" (72),
is also modelled after an earlier Harben short story character,
Abner Calihan. Like Calihan, Abner Daniel undergoes a heresy
trial. Several opponents, including his minister, attack him for his
unorthodox beliefs: "He 'lowed he didn't believe hell was any
hot place nohow, an' that he never could be made to believe that
the Lord ud create folks an' then barbecue 'em alive through all

eternity" (106). Abner uses the Bible for practical purposes: "When I'm in doubt about whether a thing's right or wrong, I generally find some Scriptural sanction fer the side I want to win" (279). At his trial, he is defended by many who have benefited from his kindness as a good neighbor, and finally exonerated. But because he sees that his beliefs are tearing apart the church, he nobly promises to "keep from shovin' my notions on folks that ain't ready fer 'em" (117). He compromises, as did Abner Calihan, but refuses to conform completely to the commands of his community when his conscience tells him such submission is wrong. Later, in *The Georgians* (1904), he finds some folks who are ready for his notions; so, not to be outdone, he preaches his good sense to them.

Possibly more memorable than Abner Daniel in this novel is another character Harben kept returning to, the uncouth, tender Pole Baker, who speaks one of the novel's best lines, which illustrates his fondness for moonshine whiskey. When urged to choose the manner of death he would select if he had to die, Pole says, "Well, boys, ef I had to go, I'd like to be melted up into puore corn whiskey an' poured through my throat tell thar wasn't a drap left of me" (299). The heroic task of recovering the Bishops' fortune is delegated to Pole. He cleverly and bravely forces a crooked banker to admit that he had embezzled his own bank and to return the twenty-five thousand dollars that the Bishops had entrusted to him. (The setting for the exciting scene in which Pole locks the kidnapped banker in his secret moonshining cave originated in Harben's earlier short story, "A Message from the Stream.") Pole is rewarded for his achievements with a prosperous farm which the Bishops give to him and his wife and seven children.

Harben's interest in phrenology, the study of bumps on the head, is present in Pole's having his head examined by a travelling phrenologist. "He made a business o' feelin' o' heads an' writin' out charts at twenty-five cents apiece. When he got to Pole's noggin he talked fer a good hour. I never heard the like. He said ef his talents had been properly directed Pole ud 'a' made a big public man. He said he hadn't run across sech a head in a month o' Sundays. He was right, you bet, an' every one o' the seven brats Pole's got is jest as peert as he is" (77). Later, another character who views Pole with admiration repeats the phrenologist's appraisal: "It's a fact. You could 'a' made some'n' out o'

yorese'f if you'd 'a' been educated, an' had a showin'" (217).
These opinions of Pole are foreshadowings of Harben's later,
more serious use of him as an illustration of the potential rise of
the poor white Southerner.

Harben modelled Pole Baker after a popular mountaineer he
had observed one day in Dalton. "He was under thirty years of
age, tall, broad-shouldered, raw-boned and coatless; his broad-
brimmed hat was torn, his shirt and trousers ragged."[30] The
intoxicated mountaineer and a soapbox temperance preacher
exchanged insults on the main street and the mountaineer ended
up on the rock pile among black convicts. But he refused to do
any work whatsoever, and his friends paid his fine, "for there was
no other recourse than for the mayor to have the prisoner
whipped, and he would not resort to that way of losing future
votes."[31] Indeed, one of the best pieces of reading in *Abner
Daniel* is the scene in which Pole is jailed for disturbing the
peace and put on a chain gang to break rock, a useless move since
Pole "didn't work a lick" (191). Like Abner, Pole appears
frequently in later Harben novels centered around life in Darley.

In *Abner Daniel* the town of Darley is used extensively for the
first time. The concrete descriptions of the town show that
Harben knew it intimately: from the village street where the law
offices and the black barber shops were located—where
everyone could leave his door open so his neighbor might run in
and take his time or his belongings—to the one splendid hotel in
town, the Johnston House, where the exclusive set gave
entertainments at which the young men voted on the question of
wearing "spike tails" or not. The intense pride and wise humor of
the mountain people of Darley are shown when a Yankee
businessman talks down to the local citizens, stating that "he and
his capital were going to dispel darkness where it had reigned
since the dawn of civilization" (296). In the fashion of true
Southwestern humor, the city slicker gets his come-uppance
when a proud Darley citizen retaliates sarcastically: "Fellow-
citizens, an' ladies an' gentlemen, we are glad to welcome
amongst us a sort of a second savior in our Sodom an' Gomorry of
crackerdom. What the gentleman with the plug hat an' spike-toe
shoes ain't a-goin' to do fer us the Lord couldn't. . . . Accordin'
to him we need 'im every hour, as the Sunday-school song puts it.
Yes, he's a-goin' to he'p us powerful an' right off" (296-97). The
citizen then goes on to completely destroy the argument of the
pretentious Yankee. Harben's mountaineers, country yokels

though they may be, are usually adept at squelching patronizing
outsiders with their wisdom and backwoods rhetoric. *Their* pride
was also obviously a source of pride for Harben.

Although the racial situation is only briefly touched upon in
this novel, Harben does allow Abner to voice an invective against
Yankee interference in what he considers a Southern problem:

> I wisht I could meet some o' them durn big Yankees that are a-sendin'
> the'r money down heer an' buildin' fine schools to educate niggers an'
> neglectin' the'r own race beca'se it fit agin 'em. You cayn't hardly beat
> larnin' into a nigger's head, an' it ud be only common-sense to spend
> money whar it ud do the most good. I 'ain't got nothin' agin a nigger
> bein' larnt to read an' write, but I cayn't stomach the'r bein' forced
> ahead o' deservin' white folks sooner 'n the Lord counted on. Them
> kind of Yankees is the same sort that makes pets o' dogs, an' pampers
> 'em up when pore white children is in need of food an' affection. (77-
> 78)

These are chilling words which immediately label Uncle Abner a
bigot, good as he is otherwise; but such attitudes prevailed then
and prevail in places now in the South, so Harben cannot be
faulted for depicting the truth, ugly as it may be.

An amusing sidelight to *Abner Daniel* was a tongue-in-cheek
article appearing in *Esquire* several years ago concerning the
language used by our American astronauts. Commander Walter
M. Schirra had exclaimed at one point in an Apollo mission that,
"You're right smack dab in the middle of the plot," and Major
Leroy Gordon Cooper shouted joyously that he had come down
"right on the old bazoo!" Amused by such language, William H.
Honan traced the words to *Abner Daniel* and Harben, "a now
completely forgotten . . . hack Victorian novelist . . . who had
an absolute genius—unrivaled before or since—for phony
colloquialisms. He could cram more 'By crackeys,' 'Tarnations,'
'Looky heres,' 'Gee whillikins' and 'Jumpin' Jehoshaphats' on a
page than Shakespeare could images or Alexander Pope rhymes.
And the public ate it up."[32] Honan noted that Harben was so
successful that it is almost impossible for presentday philologists
to determine whether anyone ever really said "Looky here" or
"Gee whillikins" before the Georgia novelist popularized such
expressions in his novels. "Harben was a sort of rhetorical Robert
Goddard of the space program, . . . and *Abner Daniel* is a
veritable glossary of space terms."[33]

V   The Substitute

Abner Daniel did not appear in Harben's novel for 1903, *The Substitute*, "a good, wholesome story that brings the smile and compels the emotional tear."[34] Harben used the Grand Hotel technique here; although there is a major plot, interest is concentrated primarily on the lives of four men who work in the office of Hiram Hillyer's cotton warehouse in Darley. Hillyer, one of the most prosperous men of Darley, is plagued with guilt about a death he caused thirty years before. He is finally absolved of blame by the dead man's mother at the end of the novel; but the strength of this guilt feeling had caused him to become the most charitable, understanding citizen in Darley. The major means of atonement for Hillyer is the education and training of George Buckley so that the younger man might become his moral substitute in the sight of Providence. Buckley is the typical sterling hero unable to declare his love for wealthy Lydia Cranston because his father is a convict. Overcoming a series of reversals in his fortune, including romantic rivalry with the governor of Georgia, Buckley, with everyone's blessings, wins the hand of Lydia after his father has been cleared of wrong-doing in an overly coincidental ending.

Hillyer's second employee, Jim Kenner, is a jovial forty-five-year-old bachelor and "the biggest man-gossiper in Darley."[35] Kenner is finally mated to Hillyer's niece, Hortense Snowden, "a rather plain girl of thirty" (16), and their awkward romance is humorously depicted. The problem of the generation gap is brought out in the life of Henry Hanks, the fourth man in the office. Hanks has never fully understood or properly handled his twenty-one-year-old son Bob, who proves himself to be a shrewd, successful businessman through his intuitive knowledge of effective theories of marketing. Bob profitably operates a local grocery store, to his father's secret delight.

Although the plot is episodic and interspersed with too many irrelevant, albeit charming, local-color yarns, and although Hillyer's scene with the mother of the man he had killed consists of the stylized, maudlin, but currently popular writing of pulp magazines, *The Substitute* is a substantial story of life in North Georgia. The older minor characters are again the most memorable, especially Mrs. Hillyer and Bascom Truitt, both rugged, bighearted, and delightful. After using Abner Daniel in his preceding novel, Harben substituted these two philosophical mountaineers to supply comic relief and to boldly aid the hero in his conquest of the heroine. Mrs. Hillyer is a meddlesome good sort who is given to Abner Daniel homilies: "Don't kick agin the pricks. . . . Ef you set down on a board with a tack on it, the harder you set the more tack you git, an' that's so with life; it's full of tacks and don't you forgit it" (58). She is devilish at times in her merciless teasing of her busybody neighbor, and shrewdly practical at other times, as in her advice to bachelor Kenner: "Don't git married, Mr. Kenner. . . . A woman will either keep yore nose to the grindstone with 'er mouth shet, or talk you to death—or both" (87). Evidences of Abner Daniel are abundant in the character of Bascom Truitt, although Bascom is more of a curmudgeon than Abner; he is a man of immediate decision and action. After conning free train passage to Atlanta, he boldly faces the governor, Buckley's cowardly rival, and actually boxes the executive's ears until the politician promises to abandon his pursuit of Lydia.

The obligatory mob scene in this novel is strongly reminiscent of the Colonel Sherburn lynch mob scene in *The Adventures of Huckleberry Finn.* Buckley faces a mob of fifty White Caps and shames them into backing down: "You are a set of cowards . . . running like a pack of wolves after a poor boy for what he said and did when he was drunk. Now clear out the last one of you!" (174). He then improbably persuades the mob to actually accept the man they were about to lynch: "George seems friendly to the cuss, an' any friend o' his is safe, as fur as I'm concerned" (175).

In this novel Harben was rather brutal in his depiction of the minor black characters, referring to them as comical "black fools" with rolling eyes or as threatening "black creatures" with suppressed malevolence. But he squarely condemned the White Caps, who had "raised hell here about a year ago, you know—whippin' niggers in Niggertown" (171). Although Harben's latent feelings of justice had not yet surfaced, there were indications that such feelings were present and forthcoming.

William Dean Howells especially liked Harben's handling of Hillyer's lifelong remorse, "not the less affecting because it is expressed in natures of primitive simplicity," and his treatment of ordinary people: "His psychological reach over the lowly levels of life to the heights where men live in the spirit is certainly not the less striking because the life is that of common

men and women."[36] The novel was a popular one—there was
even a large order for it from Australia. Harben was especially
pleased that his works were received so favorably from the other
side of the world.[37]

VI   The Georgians

In his 1904 novel, *The Georgians,* Harben resurrected the
genial old busybody, Abner Daniel, who again has his finger in
every public and private pie in Darley. Harben uses Uncle Abner
to better advantage here than he does in the book to which the
old philosopher in jeans lent his name. *The Georgians* could aptly
be titled *Abner Daniel, Super Detective,* for Abner emerges as
the major character who saves the lives of many by his
straightforward, relentless detective work. No other characters
from the previous work appear, although the Bishop family is
mentioned once when Abner explains that after their good
fortune they had moved to New York.

Si Warren, "a regular demon in human hide,"[38] has been
sentenced to hang for the murder of a man he killed in self-
defense. The only person who can save him is the witness to the
killing—who has vanished. Eric Vaughn, a young landholder, has
secretly spent thousands of dollars trying to find the witness
because Eric had loved Warren's daughter Marie many years
before. Marie had died five years earlier in New Orleans,
according to her father, who hates Eric. Eric's father, a proud old
patrician who is blindly investing all his money in a nonexistent
college for blacks, plans to disinherit his son, who he thinks is
recklessly squandering his money.

At this point Uncle Abner, with the skill of a Pinkerton
detective and the humor of a backwoods comedian, rights all
wrongs. With untiring zeal he scours the country from Texas to
New York seeking the missing witness, before eventually
producing him in time to save Si Warren. Uncle Abner also
discovers that Marie is still alive and is, in fact, a well-born lady,
having been adopted by Warren; he brings the girl to her lover's
arms. He also gleefully exposes a confidence game concerning
the black college, restores the elder Vaughn's money, and closes
the breach between father and son. Yet Uncle Abner is never
rushed for time, as there are always spare moments to chat, to
swap yarns, to preach brotherly love, to play practical jokes, and

generally to help, encourage, and love everything from man to beast that comes his way. In short, he is a thoroughly delightful character whom the reader comes to admire and love even more than in his first novel.

Many of his anecdotes, and they are again abundant, are humorously shrewd—"I sometimes think the niggers has it down about right when they sing: 'De Lawd move in er mischievous way His blunders to perform'" (40)—but he is quite serious when he talks religion to his Sunday school class—consisting of himself and two other men, both of whom admire and agree with Uncle Abner's ideas, and regard him "as a subaltern might his general in the heat of successful conflict" (165). The three dissenters from traditional religion, though mild free thinkers, are not so certain of their beliefs as to degrade the traditional worshippers: "Say what you please, boys, reason as you will, debate an' argue, an' prove an' disprove till you are black in the face, an' you won't have the speritual content that's built a fire in mightly nigh every face in this room. Them sort's got some'n to cling to; but all three of us is gropin' in a dark cave" (69).

Abner admits to the two men that he was tried for heresy several years back "beca'se I shot off my bazoo about what I thought was Scriptur'. I was havin' a good time tellin' folks about how I interpreted sacred writ, but it seems I was tramplin' the'r pet notions in the mire." So he then interprets the Bible to his willing audience anyway:

Now, fer be it from me to underrate the sacred book o' books; but, boys, grand as it is, parts of it, at least, was writ by men who didn't have much imagination. . . . The sacred book is full o' places whar the writers show they lack that particular gift. . . . Now, thar was a man mentioned in the New Testament by the name o' Lazarus. Boys, he come back from an existence that never was even imagined. He come back from death an' all death means; he'd been away three whole days an' nights; he was dead ef any man ever was, an' yet the writer that described his return never recorded that any human soul that witnessed his resurrection cared to ax 'im whar he'd been or what he'd experienced. The feller that writ about it actually put in all the little things about what Lazarus wore at the time the Great Man performed the act, but he let the subject rest right thar. The eternal problem was as important then as it is now. It was the one question every mortal wanted answered—the question as to what lay behind the veil, beyond the storms o' soul an' body. Lazarus could 'a' answered it, but nobody give 'im a chance. He

lived along like the rest after that, but the Bible writers never
mentioned that he was a man o' any particular note. Jest let that rankle
in yore minds a minute. (43, 74-76)

Liberal as he is on religion, Abner is Southern enough to be
self-righteous and stiff-necked at times concerning civil rights.
The confidence man who promotes the black college speaks to
Abner:

"But surely, Mr. Daniel, you—a man as broad and liberal as you are—
you are not going to argue that one set of human beings have the
exclusive right to occupy any portion of the face of God's earth,
keeping out and holding down another set simply because they happen
to have darker skins."
"I don't know about that," said Abner; "but I *do* believe, ef any
makin' over *has* to be done, that it will be a sight easier to make over a
few colored people that never are troublesome, until some person gits
to devilin' 'em an' incitin' 'em to disorder, than to make over a race that
never has been made over by nobody nur never will. Niggers kin be
made over *some*, ur they never would 'a' been fetched agin the'r will so
fur from home; but the puore white blood never was led about an'
dictated to, nur it never will be." (107-08)

In other words, Abner opposes compulsory civil rights because
in his eyes compulsion will not work. He believes in a middle
ground which does not exist. Though he realizes that the
Southerner is offbalance and vulnerable and that the black is the
underdog, he will not offer automatic sympathy simply because
the race is "down." From a Southern standpoint, Uncle Abner's
views are more practical than bigoted, for he realizes an
emotional condition of the entire South is involved, not simply a
legal theory and a moral idea. Yet Harben is somehow not
completely convincing in the views he gives Abner in this novel;
he had yet to make a solid stand on the racial issue.
    Since *Abner Daniel* was already a success, Harben arranged
for an Abner Daniel story, "Two Birds With One Stone," to
appear in the *Century* (May, 1905) at the same time *The
Georgians* came out, "to help both the short story and the
novel."[39] The novel was a huge success, and one critic called
Harben "a gentle realist" who demonstrated an exception to the
theory that the South lacked a sense of humor. He put Harben
alongside such Georgia humorists as A. B. Longstreet, J. J.

Hooper, and Joel Chandler Harris.[40] *Harper's Weekly* noted that in *The Georgians* Harben had mastered the art of telling yarns to perfection and called the book "wholly ingenuous and unaffected, . . . entertaining and refreshing, . . . and rich in humor."[41] Abner Daniel had succeeded again.

VII   Pole Baker

In *Pole Baker* (1905), the title character serves the same purpose Abner Daniel did; he is a folksy, crude, but wise mediator. Curiously, he is better developed and far more interesting in *Abner Daniel* than in this, his own book. Harben seemed compelled to draw Pole and his moral anecdotes into the story too much, overexposing him at times, whereas in *Abner Daniel* Pole could remain in the background and thereby become more memorable. "Old Uncle Ab" is mentioned several times in *Pole Baker* and some of his pranks are talked about, but he never appears in the book.

The chief plot concerns Nelson Floyd, a young man who has become rich and popular in Darley but who "broods over the mystery that hangs over his origin."[42] The heroine this time is not an aristocrat, but a commoner named Cynthia Porter. In the course of the surprisingly disappointing novel, Floyd discovers he is illegitimate, goes on a drunken spree (all the way to Cuba), discovers he is *not* illegitimate, wins Cynthia, loses Cynthia, and then wins her again. Harben does not handle his two main characters well; he gives them melodramatic, cliché ridden dialogue to speak, and unnatural, stilted actions to perform. The result is that the reader does not care what happens to the two lovers. Harben is overly obsessed with his familiar theme of family name and background, which may have been important in his time but is less than tolerable today.

Even the minor characters are not as interesting in this novel. Sally Baker, Pole's wife, is a spunky, likable sort, but no more so than in *Abner Daniel.* Reverend Hillhouse, Cynthia's other suitor, is a mechanical, stereotypical Ichabod Crane. Cynthia's mother is eccentric, but certainly not memorable. One exception, to a degree, is Cynthia's father, Nathan Porter, amateur inventor of a "fly flap" (fly swatter) and back scratcher. He is also a humorist of sorts: "Think o' the plumb foolishness, parson, o' layin' a man away on a silk-plush cushion after he's dead, when he's slept all his life on a common tick stuffed with corn-shucks with the stubs on 'em" (129).

It is thus up to Pole Baker to save the novel, but too much of his dialogue and actions are altered replays of happenings in the earlier books, including a reenactment of the situation in "Jim Trundle's Crisis," a short story from *Northern Georgia Sketches* in which Pole is threatened with a beating by the White Caps. Pole does speak some humorously perceptive lines, such as "Matrimony is like a sheet of ice, which, until you bust it, may cover pure, runnin' water or a stagnant mud-hole" (56), but his best qualities are the ease with which he associates with most scions in the upper ranks of society—and his refusal to allow any in these ranks to appear superior to him. When a member of the gentry patronizes him, Pole says, "I'm here to say I don't take off my hat to no man on earth" (10). The middle class, which benefits from his assistance, repays him handsomely. Just as Alan Bishop had given Pole's family a farm in *Abner Daniel*, Nelson Floyd presents him with a farm management at three thousand dollars a year as a reward for his aid. Pole is symbolic of the rise of the lower class in the South,[43] a theme Harben developed more fully three years later in *Gilbert Neal*.

After the book had become a success, the exmoonshiner who was the model for Pole angrily called on Harben in Dalton. "Look y'heer, . . . folks says you've been pokin' fun at me in a book. I don't know whether it's so or not, but I'm heer to say ef it is, me'n you'll hitch in short order."[44] Harben insisted that the man read the book and then, if he still desired it, he would give him satisfaction. When the mountaineer finished reading, he laid the book down and said sheepishly, "I don't think I kin kick. I was a little afeerd you'd made me show the white-feather, but that feller they say is like me's got a sight more grit 'an I have. Huh! he'd fight a circular saw barehanded. No, I don't think I kin kick."[45] The man had read Pole Baker's character accurately, for Pole is essentially a Southern hero, and his moral character and social rise are an optimistic prophecy of the democracy of the white South.[46] Later, this same man wrote Harben asking for a personally autographed copy of the book for his wife's Christmas present. "She's powerfully tickled over what the neighbors say about me and her being in the book. Folks used to say when you was a boy that you didn't have much sense, but I believe you had as much as anybody. It was just covered up."[47]

In the final analysis, *Pole Baker* is spirited enough to be considered adequate, and some critics hailed it as Harben's best work in fiction so far; but the overall impression was that it is not one of Harben's better novels.

VIII   Ann Boyd

In 1906 Harben published perhaps his most memorable book, *Ann Boyd.* Dedicated to William Dean Howells and set in the countryside outside Darley, this powerful novel *is* Harben's best up to this point, largely because of his extensive, realistic portrayal of his middleage heroine. As in so many of his works, the idea for the book came to Harben from a real-life experience. On a circus day in Dalton, Harben was looking for a vantage point for the parade on the crowd filled streets. He noticed a vacant veranda overlooking the street and recalled that he knew the occupant of the apartment, a widowed recluse who had bitterly survived a scandal in her youth. He reintroduced himself to her, and they had a pleasant chat. When Harben asked if he might view the parade from her veranda, a change came over her and she became furious: "So that's what you spoke to me for! . . . You are the same stripe as all the rest. I've been living in this rotten town for forty years and they all slough away from me as if I was a leper covered with sores. But the minute they want a favour like you want, they come fawning and smirking. I don't pay taxes on this property for you nor none of your sort."[48] Harben did not gain the use of her veranda, but she had "beaten a plot for a novel into the very marrow of my bones, and afterward I learned more of her life, persecution, and suffering than I was ever able to transcribe."[49]

The plot slightly resembles *The Scarlet Letter*, but, unlike Hester Prynne, Ann Boyd is completely innocent. Twenty years before, she had been accused of adultery with Colonel Preston Chester, a wealthy, dissolute landowner. Her husband Joe had divorced her and taken their daughter with him after believing the lies of Jane Hemingway, who loved Joe and was jealous of Ann's having won him. Living in isolation except for one friendly neighbor, Ann has become the wealthiest woman in the county because this very isolation has made her work hard and become shrewd in business affairs. The many years of abuse have made her bitter and cynical, and she constantly hopes for revenge:

"They are trying to drive me to the wall with their sneers and lashing tongues. But I'll show them that a worm can turn."[50] She has pure hatred in her heart for Jane—and even for Jane's daughter, Virginia, whom she does not know.

Ann befriends Luke King, a poor but bright young man whose education she finances. He eventually becomes an influential editor in Atlanta and falls in love with Virginia. Jane Hemingway discovers that she has cancer, but she cannot raise the money needed to go to Atlanta for an operation. Langdon Chester, Colonel Chester's debauched son, offers the money to Virginia if she will give herself to him. Ann overhears their conversation, and is ecstatic that her revenge against Jane can take the same form her own earlier misfortune had taken. But when Ann learns that Luke loves Virginia, she wrestles with her conscience and finally saves Virginia from Chester in a harrowing, suspenseful scene at the Chester estate. She then gives Virginia the money for Jane's operation, making the girl promise to keep it a secret.

After the operation, Jane learns of Virginia's friendship with Ann and of Ann's aid to herself and her daughter, and after a temporary railing against Ann's motives, she sees that she has lived a life of sin and courageously confesses publicly that she has been lying about Ann Boyd for over twenty years. The ending of the novel finds Luke and Virginia together, when in a highly improbable, melodramatic conclusion, a reconciliation between Ann and Joe takes place.

The exposition of past events is handled naturally, not at all forced as in some of Harben's earlier works. Harben once again shows that he is more adept at writing about the older character types than about young heroes and heroines, and makes extensive use of such characters in *Ann Boyd*. Ann herself dominates the book from the first page to the last. "Mrs. Boyd, although past fifty, showed certain signs of having been a good-looking woman. . . . Her face, even in repose, wore an almost constant frown, and this habit had deeply gashed her forehead with lines that deepened when she was angry" (1-2). She believes that the only way to fight is to hit back, which she has been doing for years. She eventually comes to see that her retaliation is as blameworthy as the antagonism of her enemies. Admitting that she can love as well as hate, "though I've done more hating in my life than loving" (272), Ann immediately bestows her maternal love on Virginia once she identifies with the girl. This decision is understandable, for Ann's own daughter, Hettie, is a selfish, hateful person, and Ann herself admits, "I don't care a snap of my finger about my *own* child. She's full grown now, and has her natural plans and aspirations, and is afraid my record will blight them" (272).

Ann is thus a completely honest woman with no pretensions whatsoever. At the end of the novel, after learning that the whole church congregation has given testimonials about her goodness—which they had suspected and doubted alternately for years—she states:

I can't possibly be any way but the way the Lord made me, and to save my life I can't feel grateful. They all just seem to me like a lot of spoilt children that laugh or cry over whatever comes up. Somehow a testimonial from a congregation like that, after a lifetime of beating me and covering me with slime, seems more like an insult than a compliment. They think they can besmirch the best part of my life, and then rub it off in a minute with good intentions and a few words. Why, it was the same sort of whim that made them all follow Jane Hemingway like sheep without a leader. I don't hate 'em, you understand, but what they do or say simply don't alter my feelings a speck. I have known all along that I had the right kind of—character, and to listen to their sniffling testimony on the subject would seem to me like—well, like insulting my own womanhood. (367-68)

Such statements reveal Ann Boyd to be a practical, proud woman who sees people and life as they really are; she will not be taken in by sham, despite its being cloaked with goodness. William Dean Howells agreed that she is an outstanding person: "I should not wish to instance Ann Boyd . . . as a faultlessly heroic character, but it is hard to keep from calling her sublime in the successive developments of her nature, which are always toward the light given her by experience. What one may safely say is that she is a great creature."[51]

The other older characters are not so fully drawn as Ann, but they are equally striking. Jane Hemingway is a vindictive, selfish woman afraid of death and disgrace. Her bachelor brother-in-law, Sam Hemingway, is both humorous in his caustic comments about women and disgusting in his ignorance of the sufferings of others and in his overweening concern for his own comforts. Mary Waycroft, Ann's kind, gossipy friend and confidante, loyally stands by Ann throughout the years. Brother Bazemore,

102   WILL N. HARBEN

the pastor of the local church, has become a vehement "man of God" who is full of hate and his own power in the community; in him Harben offers a realistic portrayal of a backwoods religious fanatic. Finally, Joe Boyd, Ann's husband, once the dashing swain whom Ann won over Jane, is now an impotent, unsuccessful shell of a man. That Harben felt compelled to reconcile him with Ann at the end is the weakest point of the novel.

There are no derogatory remarks about or condescensions to blacks in this book at all. Harben again showed his maturity toward this subject; as a successful author, he did not seem to be giving in to what was expected of a Southern writer. Ann, for example, does not pay the black people who worked for her with old clothing, or secondgrade meat or grain. "On Ann's place it was different. At the end of each day, hard, jingling cash was laid into their ready palms, and it was symbolic of the freedom which years before had appeared in name only" (154).

Harben had already begun incorporating earlier stories and novels into later works, and *Ann Boyd* best exemplifies this practice. He introduced most of his story "The Tender Link" into the plot line of this novel almost verbatim. The name of the hero, Luke King, remains unchanged,[52] and there is even identical wording in dialogue and description. Other similarities include the stepfather-stepson conflict, the descriptions of the cabin, the moving reunion scene between mother and son, the fact that Luke King becomes a successful writer, and Luke's buying a plantation for his family.

Ann Boyd was critically and popularly successful. In 1911, Lucille LaVerne dramatized it, and the play premiered in New York City at Wallack's Theater on March 31, 1913, with Miss LaVerne enacting the title role herself; it was a shortlived production.[53] Harben, who had no hand in the dramatization, did enjoy watching rehearsals of the play in New York. A motion picture was made of the novel in 1927.[54]

The review of the novel in the New York *Times* was unenthusiastic,[55] but the *Literary Digest*'s critique typified the overwhelmingly favorable reviews. After commending Harben for spurning the traditions and paraphernalia of contemporary novelists, this review praised the unromantic setting, the flesh-and-blood characters, and the rude and unpretentious story. "In some portions of the book the writer has succeeded in imparting a suggestion of the rude pathos and unaffected sentiment that we associate with the peasant paintings of Millet."[56] More recently, Robert Bush complimented the book on its regional and parochial levels but broadened his appreciation of it to a universal level, suggesting that it makes a statement about humanity rather than about life in a particular community: "We are more interested in Ann as a human being than as a Northern Georgia farm woman, and it is the complication in her character that gives the novel the touch of profundity. Her misfortune has embittered her and makes her live with vindictiveness until she is released from the bonds made by calumny. The moral burden of the novel is the old idea that evil begets evil, that only goodness and generosity destroy it."[57]

Anyone who reads *Ann Boyd*, certainly one of Harben's strongest novels, would agree with the *Independent* that "the author has met the demands of literary art in the construction of his book."[58]

IX   Mam' Linda

Having avoided the controversial racial issue as a major theme for several years, Harben returned to it with a vengeance in his 1907 novel, *Mam' Linda*. In a letter to Joel Chandler Harris, written while the novel was still in the planning stages, Harben confided that it would be a simple, strong story showing the actual conditions existing between the races in Georgia. "I want to rouse sympathy for the negroes, for the better class of whites who love and understand them. . . . It will show, perhaps for the first time in print, the awful suffering of an innocent and long pursued negro accused of crime, the suffering of his anxious people and the masters who love and respect them."[59] Harben was duly proud of this novel. Though his characters are necessarily patronizing at times, he had found himself in relation to the racial problem, and succeeded in making his message of equality clear and precise.

Carson Dwight, a young lawyer of Darley, is the character set in isolation from much of his community—especially the mountaineers—because of his unpopular belief that the black man is being treated unfairly, that he has certain rights which he is not able to use. Dwight has some followers in the town, but by and large the citizens think he has no chance of winning the election for state representative. The White Caps, this time

depicted as a renegade mob, beat some boisterous blacks one
night, and several days later, the leader of the mob and his wife
are found murdered. The prime suspect is Pete Warren, Mammy
Linda and Uncle Lewis's son. Pete is about to be lynched by the
mob when Dwight persuades them to imprison the young black
instead. Before another mob breaks into the jail to take Pete
again, Dwight and his friends hide him. Although the real killer is
eventually found, the mob is not yet appeased; Dwight therefore
takes Pete on a perilous journey to Chattanooga for safekeeping;
during this journey he again uses his powers of persuasion to
keep still another mob from killing both Pete and himself.
(Harben made ample use of his by now familiar mob scenes in
this book.) Dwight later kills his arch enemy in self-defense, and
after he is acquitted and hailed as the hero of the town, wins the
election. He also wins Helen Warren, his next-door neighbor,
who forgives him for his earlier days of debauchery, a trait that
seems typical of some Harben heroes—they must sow their wild
oats before they can become truly successful. Why Harben
called the book *Mam' Linda* is a puzzle, because she is not even
an important minor character. Novels with characters' names as
titles were popular then, but this title weakens an otherwise
powerful, hard-hitting story with a message. In her few brief
appearances, Mam' Linda, who had been happy in slavery and
now is disoriented and unable to adjust, seems to contradict the
novel's strong theme.

Pole Baker is reintroduced to the Darley series, but his role
here is less important than in the other books. He is a rough-and-
ready supporter of Dwight's, who at the end saves the day once
more when he persuades the mother of the man Dwight killed to
testify against her dead son. He remains a hero to the citizens of
Darley and obviously to Harben himself.

Other characters are well depicted, but a hill matron who has
only two scenes in the entire book stands out as one of the
strongest, most memorable characters in Harben's parade of
mountain women; she also voices Harben's message more clearly
than any of the other characters. Mrs. Jabe Parsons is a forceful,
outspoken woman who frees Pete from the sheriff and his deputy
after they first capture him. Before she acts, she states, "The
nigger that did that job was some scamp that's fur from the spot
by this time, and not a boy . . . with the best old mammy and
daddy that ever had kinky heads. . . . A nigger will talk back an'

act surly on his deathbed if he's mad. That's all the way they have of defendin' theirselves. If Pete hadn't talked some after the lashin' he got from them men, thar'd 'a' been some'n wrong with him. Now, you let 'im loose."[60] Then she acts: "Suddenly, without warning even to the slightest change of facial expression, she grasped the end of the shot-gun the man held, and whirled him round like a top. 'Run, boy!' she cried. 'Run for the woods, and God be with you!' " (103-04).

Mrs. Parsons appears again toward the end of the novel as a spokeswoman for her oppressed sisters at a political rally. After Dan Wiggin, Dwight's opponent, spits out his racist venom, Mrs. Parsons, the fires of contempt burning in her eyes, takes the stand and speaks, completely defiant, forthright, and powerful in her delivery and rhetoric:

"Listen to me, men, women and children!" she thundered, in a voice that was as steady and clear in resonance as a bell. "If there was ever a crafty, spider-like politician on earth you have listened to him spout today. He's picked out the one big sorespot in your kind natures and he's punched it, and jabbed it, and lacerated it with every sort of thorn he could stick into it, till he gained his aim in makin' you one and all so blind with rage at the black race that you are about to overlook the good in yore own. . . . I'm just a plain woman, but I read papers an' I've thought about it a lot. We hear some white folks say that the education the niggers are now gettin' is the prime cause of so much crime amongst the blacks—they say this in spite of the fact that it is always the uneducated niggers that commit the rascality. No, my friends, it ain't education that's the cause, it is the *lack* of it. Education ain't just what is learnt in schoolbooks. It is anything that makes folks higher an' better. . . . So I say, teach 'em the difference between right an' wrong, an' then let 'em work out their salvation. . . . *But!* wait a minute, think! How can you possibly teach 'em what law an' order is without knowin' a little about it yourselves? How can you learn a nigger what justice means when he sees his brother, son, or father, shot dead in his tracks or hung, like a scare-crow to the limb of a tree because some lower grade black man a hundred miles off has committed a dastardly deed?" (303-08)

Compare Mrs. Parsons's speech with Abner Daniel's diatribes against the black man. She represents the coming order of mountain folk who go beyond their prejudices and see the injustices done to the black—the same feelings Harben seemed to have owned all along but never expressed with any conviction until this novel. In the two scenes in which she appears, Mrs. Parsons leaves such an indelible impression that she is the one character who lingers in the reader's mind long after the book has been read.

There is a powerful, realistic chapter in which a "queer, secret meeting of negroes in the town" (140) takes place. Here Harben shows understanding and compassion for the feelings of the black. In an effort to convince the other blacks present to unite and bring to justice the real killer, an educated black preacher says, "We are being sorely tried, tried almost past endurance, but the God of the white man is the God of the black. Through a dark skin the light of a pure heart shines as far in an appeal for help towards the throne of Heaven as through a white" (142). Then a black barber tells of an Atlanta newspaper editorial: "Brother black man, dat editor said dat de white race had tried de whiplash, de rope, en de firebrand fer forty years en de situation was still as bad as ever. . . . He said it was time ter blaze er new trail, er trail dat hain't been blazed befo'—er trail of love en forgiveness en pity, er trail de Lord Jesus Christ would blaze ef he was here in de midst o' dis struggle" (143). The preacher then convinces everyone present that the prevalent view of protecting *all* their black brothers, guilty as well as innocent, "may be the one that has kept colored people from being more active in the legal punishment of their race" (150). The blacks do unite and track down the murderer. The chapter is an exciting, absorbing one, dealing with serious, dedicated blacks trying to better themselves and to find a way out of their social predicament.

James Faller wrote a dramatization of *Mam' Linda* entitled *The Hotheads.* It premiered at the Cort Theater, New York City, on February 10, 1925, after many legal entanglements with publishers and producers. Mr. Hatcher Hughes, a Southern friend of Harben's and a firm believer in the theme of the book, aided Faller in revising the play.[61] Most of the criticism of the drama was favorable, and the play was well received on Broadway.

President Theodore Roosevelt, whom the Harbens had already met at a reception in New York, had spoken many kind words about *Ann Boyd* in a letter to Harben, but he was particularly impressed with the tolerant picture of the race problem in *Mam' Linda*. Since the country was beset with similar problems at the time, the President invited Harben, along with other literary men, to the White House for a luncheon to discuss some points suggested by the story.[62] Kate Harben, not a Roosevelt fan, was disappointed that her brother had given up his Southern prejudices. "After this, the peculiar blend of red, white and blue in the Southern democratic groups did not shine out in Will's work," she wrote, implying that Harben had prostituted himself by falling in with the interests of "Big Business."[63] But Harben finally had expressed himself passionately and unequivocally on an issue on which formerly he had been ambiguous. He knew that his liberal father would have been proud of the stand he had taken, for he dedicated the book to his memory.

X   Gilbert Neal

Harben's novel for 1908 was *Gilbert Neal,* a solidly satisfying story and one of his most complex: he smoothly integrated several subplots into the thread of the main one. Gilbert Neal is a hard-working, lower class farmer who is considered a "poky old drudge" by his younger, more reckless brother Dave.[64] Gilbert has already bailed Dave out of jail twice in his life, and the younger brother is about to go to prison unless Gilbert again pays his fine. Gilbert refuses, and the young men's realistic father encourages his older son to stand behind his convictions; his mother and sister, however, urge him to mortgage the farm and save Dave again. When his sister, Lucille, leads him to believe his failure to save his brother will jeopardize her chances for marrying Graham Peters, Gilbert finally relents. Actually, Lucille is seeing the local pastor, Lawrence Tidwell, whose long-suffering wife Martha has always been a staunch defender of Gilbert. Dave knows about Lucille's affair with Tidwell and is threatening to expose them if she does not persuade Gilbert to pay his fine. After his release, Dave leaves Darley to make his fortune in the west.

A drought ruins Gilbert's crops, and he takes a job as clerk-manager of Stephen Daggart's general store in Springtown, a village outside Darley, where he is a great success. Daggart, a fat, jovial old widower, is searching for a new wife; he suffers one misadventure after another scouring the countryside for a prospective bride. Laura Tidwell, the pastor's calculating, possessive sister who has already been rejected by Gilbert, takes up with the foolish but delightful Daggart, and the two marry, she solely for his money. When Daggart dies at the end of the book, she marries the now successful and rich Dave, and the two plan a lifetime of high living. Meanwhile, Tidwell plans to elope with Lucille, but Martha discovers the plot and thwarts it before Lucille has been "wronged." Tidwell is accidentally killed, and Lucille and Peters eventually marry. After Gilbert buys Daggart's store, he and Martha seem to be on the way to the altar themselves.

All the characters are well developed and realistic, but one minor character again stands out: Jim Carden, who had appeared briefly in *The Georgians* as a member of Abner Daniel's school of individuality. Carden has graduated to become the Springtown community's Abner; he "was noted throughout the countryside as the only local individual bold enough to declare open opposition to current religious beliefs, which views he was permitted to voice only through his unfailing sense of humor and a fairly sound philosophy on all topics" (1-2). Like Abner, Carden is wise and observant; he is one of the first to see the hypocrisy and cruelty in Tidwell. He is even Abner-like in his twisting of biblical proverbs: "Cast thy bread upon the waters, go hungry, and let the mud-turtles have a feast" (28).

The Neal brothers are two of Harben's illustrations of the industrious nature of the lower classes in the aftermath of the decline of the higher classes once slavery was banned. They represent the rise of the poor whites. Both are ambitious and dissatisfied with their old poverty, but Gilbert is willing to work hard to earn his respectability, while Davé is not: "Gil's a drudge—a plodding slave. His sort are necessary to the progress of the world, but above him are the men who live by their wits, and ride in palace-cars, and enjoy, by George! enjoy the fat of the land" (55). Indeed, they both succeed in their goals. Dave, the inferior brother, becomes rich through the exercise of the very talents which had so often gotten him into trouble, but the hero, Gilbert, retains his self-respect and succeeds in a quieter, more modest way in the land he loves: "I've made up my mind that I'll live and die here in these mountains, and I can make a good living out of this business" (354). Harben's view of the new Southern morality is that the poor whites with an instinctive sense of honor and a sense of right that spring from their conscience rather than from a code will eventually be solidly middle class in another generation.[65]

While not one of Harben's very best, *Gilbert Neal* is a worthy novel. The *Nation* thought the book delightfully melodramatic, and made some general comments which accurately characterize the majority of Harben's novels: "Mr. Harben's work represents a sincere impulse to express the life of simple people in Georgia, the life with which he is evidently most familiar. His method is movingly ingenious; he writes not only of the people but from the people. Hence, his acceptableness to the popular reader. There is no nonsense about him, no condescension from the sophisticated to the uncouth."[66]

XI   The Redemption of Kenneth Galt

Unfortunately, Harben began to be inconsistent, for his next novel, *The Redemption of Kenneth Galt,* published in 1909, is pure nonsense. Although the New York *Times* review of the book was mildly favorable,[67] the *Nation* was mercilessly accurate in its critique, calling it a trashy book with astonishingly little excuse for existing. "The plot and characters are as hackneyed as the title and quality of the English."[68] The novel does not succeed because of effusive sentimentality and because Harben concentrated not on uneducated mountaineers, about whom he wrote so naturally, but on a group of artificial, upperclass aristocrats.

Wealthy Kenneth Galt has ruined and deserted a simple village maiden who has shielded him at the expense of another man's reputation. Six years later, Galt admits his guilt and persuades the maiden, who now loves another man, to marry him in order to give their precocious five-year-old son an unblemished name. Honorable as Harben's moral may be, it is of questionable value. And the overtones of *The Scarlet Letter* are this time more unintentionally comic than tragic. There are subplots concerning the cynical Galt's conversion to faith, a swindler's conversion to honesty, a cold father's conversion to warmth toward his son, and the town doctor's saintly virtues which are never in need of conversion. None of it works for Harben this time, however. William Dean Howells kindly stated that Harben was built for truer work, that the book affected him "like a labor done at the suggestion of ill-advised friends who wish their novelist to prove himself capable of higher art than that highest art of all, which is the realization of genuine life on the levels so mistakenly supposed to be low."[69] It is a book best forgotten.

XII   Dixie Hart

Harben more than redeemed himself for *Kenneth Galt* the following year with the publication of *Dixie Hart,* which justified Howells's opinion that year that Harben was the best of the national American localists.[70] Dedicated to the late Richard Watson Gilder, "whose kindly appreciation of the character of 'Dixie Hart' was my inspiration in writing the book,"[71] it is Harben's most charming story.

Alfred Henley, a hard-working storekeeper unhappily married to Hettie, a woman who never ceases mourning for her former husband, is a neighbor and close friend to Dixie Hart, an equally hard-working young woman who runs her farm alone and cares for her invalid mother and aunt. Alf is resigned to his lot in life, but the more he admires Dixie for her stamina and practical sense, the more he is attracted to her. When a mail order romance for Dixie fails, he determines to find a husband for her in the person of a fellow merchant in a neighboring town. This match also humorously but completely fails. In the end, the two principals are free to marry when Hettie's first husband, believed dead, returns after she has conveniently inherited a fortune.

The worth of the novel lies not in the plot, which is slight, but in the fascinating, ingratiating characters of Dixie Hart and Alf Henley. They are people the reader cares about, and along with Abner Daniel, Pole Baker, and Ann Boyd, are the best delineated of Harben's principal mountaineers. Dixie is a young version of Ann Boyd without the latter's bitterness and martyred attitude. She accepts life as it is and makes the best of all situations: "I know what I am well enough. I was born with a load on me, and I'm going to tote it till I get to a dumping place" (43). She is strong, stern, but patient with everyone, especially her difficult mother and aunt. Refreshingly forthright and direct, she often makes Abner Daniel-like witticisms: "As a general thing the marriage seems to rest on a big cake of ice, and overheated couples catch colds that make 'em sniff the rest of their lives"

(155). Her droll and original speech is typically backwoods, never forced: "I'd make a sensible man a good wife, and I'd do my part; but I'll be hanged if I'll walk up to him wearing a 'For Sale' tag" (133). Taken altogether, she is a wonderfully honest heroine.

Even before Dixie and Alf admit they are romantically interested in each other, the relationship between them is a warm, understanding camaraderie. Alf is a strong man, but unlike typical Harben heroes, he is humorous, a wheeler-dealer on occasion, and talks like a mountaineer instead of a prep school dandy. He deals with his dour wife firmly, shrewdly but with understanding, and he shows his compassion by allowing the parents of his wife's first husband to live with them. Jason Wrinkle, his step-father-in-law, admits that he likes Alf better than he did his own son. Wrinkle, a cantankerous, mischievous old man, is another delightful character in the novel, with his long stories and his practical jokes.

Harben's model for Dixie was a mountain maid he talked with once while waiting for a train in Dalton. He had already met her in his countryside rambles and been struck by her courage and thrift, for she was supporting a half-blind mother by planting and selling produce. At the station she confided to Harben that she was going to Atlanta to marry a man she had never met. A year later in Dalton he saw her again selling her produce, and she explained why she was back: "That thing was no go. . . . I didn't like 'im; he wasn't my style at all. . . . Why, he was actually greasy. . . . Nobody about here knows of that caper. Don't give me away. It might spoil my chances. I'm going to get married some day, but I have no idea when or who to."[72] Harben admitted that he should have bought all her produce that day at a higher price than she had ever received, for she became first the "Sprightly Heroine" of his *Harper's Weekly* short story (December 16, 1905) and later Dixie Hart herself. Dixie's episode with her pen pal suitor is based on the real story.

Several totally captivating chapters in *Dixie Hart* originated in Harben's short story, "The Sale of the Mammoth Western" (*Century*, November, 1907). In the novel Alf buys an old circus and sells each item at a profit. Finally Dixie herself buys the last item from him, the old lion's cage, and sells it at one hundred percent profit. Alf has met his match in bargaining; he is justifiably proud of her.

Besides being moving and human, the novel is supremely

humorous on many occasions. Harben showed signs of being a
first rate humorist of the Mark Twain type. Jason Wrinkle's
description of a funeral is as original and funny as Huck Finn's
description of Peter Wilks's funeral. At another time, the
uneducated Dixie and Alf wrestle long and painfully with the
arch-demon of the school-going world, fractions: "Sixty is two-
thirds of what number?" (335-37).

Although *Dixie Hart* is not as well known as some of Harben's
other books—*Abner Daniel, Pole Baker,* and *Ann Boyd* have far
surpassed it in popularity—it deserves to rank at the very top
because it is one of the most honest, entertaining novels he ever
wrote. It represented a grand climax to a decade of realistic
writing about primitive people with their own set of ideals and
standards. That most of these novels were brought out in cheap
editions for display and sale at railway newstands, the equivalent
of presentday paperbacks, is testimony to their popularity.[73]
Though Harben did not sustain the quality of his works of these
years during the next decade, he left a distinguished mark as a
literary artist.

CHAPTER 5

Literary Decline: 1910-1920

WITH one notable exception and several minor ones, the final decade of Harben's literary career was a disappointing one. He continued to be as popular as ever with lay readers, and he still averaged a novel a year, but he also began excessively to reuse old ideas, to detach himself too frequently from the mountain region of North Georgia, and to concentrate on romantic trivia. The result was a marked decline in the literary quality and significance of his work.

I *The Virginia Demarest Novels*

In 1910 and 1911, Harben wrote two inconsequential novels, both published by Harper and Brothers, under the pseudonym of Virginia Demarest. Why he chose a woman's name is a mystery, but his daughter reports that "he felt the books weren't up to his calibre, so he used this name to write trashier books."[1] In a tongue-in-cheek letter to one of the Harper editors, Harben himself wrote, "I see you have announced Miss Demarest's new book in a nice way. She writes me that if you only will push 'The Fruit of Desire' up to a good audience that she has in her head a cracking good sequel to it which—in that case—would make a big hit and make money for you both. I don't care particularly about booming other writers, but Miss Demarest is a nice, virtuous lady, and I would like to see her efforts meet with success."[2] Actually, these novels mark the beginning of the decline of Harben's career.

In the first novel, *The Fruit of Desire*, Harben regressed to the stilted sentimentality of his second book, *A Mute Confessor*. The hero and heroine, John Kenton and Edith Strode, both outcasts in a small Kentucky town, run away together and settle in New York City. Their relationship is pristinely proper. Though Edith

113

fears that they will become slaves to gross passion, they finally wed. These fears grow after their marriage: "She forced herself to be cold to her husband's embraces, looking upon the poor fellow's natural fondness as the sinister thing which was ultimately to separate them."[3] During her pregnancy Edith leaves Kenton, loses her baby, but wins back her husband through the interference of a friend, who tells Kenton, "She thinks your life and hers, before marriage, was the only perfect one. She hopes you will be willing to let it be that way—exactly that way" (331). Kenton agrees, and the two are reunited in their "Garden of Eden—the Eden which was God's ideal. No one would have asked for more who valued the beautiful things of the spirit" (297).

Had Harben admitted to the writing of the book, his respectable reputation could have been ruined, for it makes for the sort of reading adolescent schoolgirls enjoy and weep over. Neither characters nor situations ring true, dialogue and descriptions are trite, and the conclusion is strained, unnatural, and unbelievable. The New York *Times* comment was accurate: "The novel, as a whole, fails through the author's utterly distorted view of human nature and of what makes for the real ascendancy of the spirit."[4]

Nobody's, the second Virginia Demarest work, is not, as Harben had promised, a sequel to *The Fruit of Desire,* but it has all the earmarks of a Harben novel. Basically a reworking of *White Marie,* with a happy ending, it also contains elements of his other works. The New York *Times* gave this novel a generally favorable review, "though it is a bit young-ladyish in its manner of telling and in its ideas."[5] In fact, the language and descriptions are so grossly overdone and the characters are so stereotypical—given to all too familiar breastbeating, weeping, and suffering—that the book becomes a dismal failure.

Gordon Hartley, New York banker visiting his sister's plantation in Tennessee, sets out to prove that Celeste, beautiful daughter of a black slave ("a lamb in a fold of black sheep"),[6] is really white and aristocratic. This he accomplishes: when Celeste saves his life after he is bitten by a rattlesnake (a duplication of a scene in *White Marie*); after he talks his way out of a lynching (a duplication of near lynch scenes in many Harben books); after he and Celeste cling perilously to a cliff (a duplication of a scene in *A Mute Confessor*); after he slowly and carefully unravels the clues leading to Celeste's true identity (a duplication of Minard Hendricks's techniques); and through some of the most banal dialogue ever written (mercifully, not a duplication of anything Harben had ever done, even in *The Redemption of Kenneth Galt*). Were it not intended seriously, such dialogue would be comical: "I'll lift the cloud from her, rescue her from the shackles which rasp her gentle spirit if it is in the power of man to do it. She is wronged. I don't know exactly how, but she hasn't had a fair deal" (111).

The Fruit of Desire and *Nobody's* are inferior potboilers in all respects. Fortunately, "Virginia Demarest" wrote no other novels.

II   Jane Dawson

Harben returned to the grass roots with the publication of *Jane Dawson* in 1911. The book's heroine, like Ann Boyd, has been isolated and ostracized by the rest of her North Georgia community; her sin is that in her youth she had an illegitimate son, George, who is now a quick-thinking, hard-working young man. But Jane Dawson is even more bitter and cynical than Ann Boyd ever was. She has completely turned her back on the religious beliefs of her community and has become a severe agnostic: "I threatened God, who I held responsible for my plight. I swore on my knees, with my hands clasped in agony, that if help didn't come I'd be an enemy to Him and His as long as the breath of life was in me."[7] She has influenced the beliefs of her son, although the latter's agnosticism is tempered with reason and compassion.

George's father is Silas Dwight, a neighbor whose wife, Sarah, knows of her husband's sin and viciously uses this knowledge to get her own way. She is a ruthless social climber who pushes their son, Olin, into becoming a preacher. Both George and Olin love Myra Chapman, who prefers George but believes in the simple religion that Olin preaches. Much of the book is an argument between the religious fundamentalism of the country people and the rational belief which attempts to reconcile faith with reason, represented by George.

The guilt ridden Silas perceives that his preference for his spoiled but well-meaning legitimate son over his deserving but illegitimate son is unfair and finally confesses his sin to George, who forgives and accepts his father. Jane, who discovers that she is dying, to alleviate George's bearing the brunt of her sin, insincerely joins the church again. But she cannot accept the belief in a life after death—one of Harben's own overwhelming questions—until in a vision on her deathbed she is assured of an everlasting life. She thus dies peacefully, and the novel ends with George and Myra reconciling their differences and leaving Georgia for a new life in Oregon.

Spiritual unrest and growing religious issues of the day yielded an abundance of social-gospel novels. In *Jane Dawson* Harben followed this trend of his time, but he also tried to concretize the religious problems that haunted him throughout his life. Like Edwin Arlington Robinson and T. S. Eliot, he was searching for something to believe in, while his rational self told him there was nothing. Yet his inner being maintained that there had to be some final truth, for life would be unbearable otherwise. Eliot found his answer in the Church of England, Harben in the Unitarian Church—like Tom Mell, the most outspoken agnostic in *Jane Dawson.* Mell eventually finds merit and consolation in this denomination which advocates reason; Harben became a Unitarian after he had lived in New York for several years.

George Dawson represents Harben's viewpoints. Echoing Stanley Clayton in *Almost Persuaded,* George stands midway between the conventional religious views of his community and the harsh, agnostic views of his mother. When he tries to convince Myra that inflexibly orthodox believers in every age have bitterly fought advancement, he cites Ralph Waldo Emerson in defending his unpopular stand: "You can tell me with all that force and sweet sympathy that I ought to stifle my convictions as to truth, while Emerson says it is a man's duty to cry his honest opinions from a housetop. I want people to believe as you do who get comfort out of it, but there must be something higher and deeper for those who simply can't accept the strictly orthodox creed" (124).

Myra disagrees with George, arguing that he makes "a mere flesh-and-blood pygmy of the only-begotten Son of God" (205). Myra, who finds comfort in her orthodox religion and has the most steadfast faith of any character in the book, is the devout type Harben could admire. She even admits, "I have my simple religious faith, but I am not so narrow as to think your way of thinking will keep you back" (265).

Jane herself has sternly turned against any sort of religion, and

her harshness is shown in her first appearance when she shouts to
her hated neighbor, Sarah Dwight,

You are a purty thing . . . to bring holy messages to any one. Huh! Your
fat, wobbling body right now fairly drips with the slime of hell. Your
tongue is forked and full of venom. You ain't here to do me no good
turn. I know you. You are the foulest snake that ever coiled under
weeds and grass to strike the helpless. A lot of good your prayers and
psalm-singing will do you in this life or any other! . . . You—you
meddlesome hypocrite! . . . If you was not such a coward and sneak, I'd
climb that fence and jerk every rag from your filthy carcass. (11-13)

But by the end of the novel, Jane becomes convinced of a
beautiful life after death; her bitterness subdued, she dies with
an inner tranquillity.

Presenting the various religious beliefs of the North Georgia
mountain people who represent society's conflict with religious
issues, *Jane Dawson* is one of the few novels of reasonable quality
that Harben wrote during his last decade.

III   Paul Rundel

Harben followed *Jane Dawson* in 1912 with an excessively
morbid story called *Paul Rundel*, loosely based on an early short
story, "John Bartow." With this novel he began his practice of
dividing his works into parts, to signify lapses of years in the
narrative. In part I Paul Rundel is a sullen youth who supports his
ill father and flirtatious mother by working for Iim Hoag, richest
man in Grayson, near Darley. Paul's father dies after vowing to
kill his neighbor Jeff Warren for trying to take his wife away
from him; in a rage Paul then shoots Warren and runs away,
thinking the man is dead.

Part II opens seven years later when Paul, now an upstanding
figure of saintly disposition, returns to discover that Warren had
recovered, married Paul's mother, and left the state. Paul, a
supremely uninteresting hero, becomes the efficient manager of
Hoag's enterprises and an uncommonly positive influence over
the entire community: he saves Hoag's older son from a life of
sin, pacifies a lynch mob, abolishes the Ku Klux Klan from the
region, supports his mother and Warren when they return in a
fallen state, comforts and converts Ethel Mayfield, Hoag's niece,
while winning her love in the process.

The subplot concerning Jim Hoag is far more interesting

because Hoag is a more complex, vulnerable figure than Paul is. Although he is a power in his community, Hoag is secretly the leader of the Klan and is responsible for vigilante lynchings and riots. His aloof handling of his older son Henry has caused Henry to lead a dissolute life until Paul saves him; but his love for his younger son Jack (who practices the lost art of making mud pies) is tender and telling. Eventually Hoag's own men in the Klan— the men whose fanatic ideas he had molded—turn against him, and he is finally killed by black vigilantes who discover that he has been their chief persecutor.

Harben strongly shows the injustices to blacks and the evil of the mob law the Klan advocates. "This is a white man's country, Cap, an' we ain't goin' to let a few lazy niggers run it. . . . The rope, the torch, an' our spooky garb an' masks are the only things niggers are afraid of." [8] The "niggers" in this story turn the tables on the Klan, though, and counter with the Klan's own methods. Their revenge is told almost with glee by Harben; his racial attitude remains as firm as it was five years before in *Mam' Linda*.

Although there is some honest realism in *Paul Rundel*, Harben's handling of the unsympathetic hero, the stilted sentimentality of too many scenes, and the unrelievedly somber tone of the book result in a weak novel.

IV   The Desired Woman

Harben did not fare any better with his 1913 novel. Although the New York *Times* called it "an eminently satisfying story"[9] and the *Nation* complimented it for its "engaging crudity,"[10] *The Desired Woman* shows a marked decline in Harben's writing powers. His style is more wooden and plodding than in most of his previous works. Extensive revision of the whole novel would have lessened the monotony of excessively melodramatic situations and overripe prose. As usual, the few scenes among the mountain folk are far more natural and realistic than the more frequent ones among the Atlanta society set.

Part I tells of Dick Mostyn, a jaded Atlanta banker who vacations in the North Georgia mountains and falls in love with schoolteacher Dolly Drake. He returns to Atlanta where, because he lacks strength of character, he marries socialite Irene Mitchell and resigns himself to life with her in Atlanta. Meanwhile, Dolly is comforted by Jarvis Saunders, Mostyn's more stable partner, who owns a plantation in the Georgia hills.

Part II opens five years later. Mostyn's loveless marriage is a failure, while Saunders has moved to the mountains to be near Dolly, whom he still loves. After Mostyn's wife commits suicide and his son dies, the banker is left with nothing but regrets for the life he has lived. When he is rejected by Dolly, who now loves Saunders, he gives his fortune away and leaves for California with an itinerant preacher who awakens in him a realization of the futility and worthlessness of his former mode of life. In the short epilogue Mostyn returns six years later a changed man. He has found peace with himself after much suffering, and visits Dolly, Saunders, and their two children.

Harben's feelings on the superiority of rural life over urban life and on what is now called women's liberation are prominent in the novel. The simplicity and unspoiled atmosphere of the mountains supply a tonic to the soul of the weak-willed Mostyn; country life is "Nature's balm for all ills."[11] Dolly argues that the constant activity of city life is hollow and valueless, and the tramp preacher, in persuading Mostyn to resist materialism, says, "The city is no better suited to real happiness than a foundry is for roses to bloom in. If you want to breathe God's breath, . . . throw this dusty grind off and go out into nature" (303). Throughout the book Harben echoes Thoreau in urging for a simpler, more natural life.

The two female characters, Dolly and Irene, symbolize the "new women" of the day. Dolly avidly champions women's equality: "The men don't *want* you to get up-to-date. . . . They think at the bottom of their hearts that women have skulls as thick as a pine board. . . . They don't know that some of the most advanced thinkers in the world are now claiming that intuition is the greatest faculty given to the human race and that woman has the biggest share of it" (87–92). Even Irene, the unloved wife, is her own woman: "You men . . . expect us women to stay at home and be as humdrum as hens in a chicken house. You are to have your fun and come home and have us wives pet you and pamper you up for another day of delight" (226). Through these women, Harben shows himself to be quite modern in his advocacy of women's rights.

Despite such valid ideas and a potential for a strong story, Harben's obviously hasty execution, his erratic style, and the maudlin situations make *The Desired Women* a careless production.

V   The New Clarion

Perhaps realizing that he was getting too far from the
characters who had succeeded for him in the past, Harben
resurrected Abner Daniel and Pole Baker for his 1914 novel, *The
New Clarion*, with the result being a substantial book in the old
Harben tradition. Abner, again the principal character, now
about seventy years of age, is as ingratiating as ever; he retains
his home-spun philosophy and willingness to help friends. He still
delights in shocking people ("The reason I know Darwin is right
about his big evolution idea is that the older I git the more
comfort I git out o' bein' like a wild animal now an' then"),[12] and
several citizens still consider him "Hell's chief agent" (86), but
he has mellowed considerably in his religious views and is almost
orthodox with his advice. Most of his community would agree
with Pole: "Ab, you are the best all-round link betwixt this world
and the next that I ever run across, an' ef I ever git to heaven it
will be by hangin' on to yore coat-tail" (343).

Pole himself is now in his mid-forties and remains a loyal friend
to those who need him. No explanation is given concerning the
plantations he was provided with in the other novels; we find
him again in a reduced state and still drinking. He is also once
more a peacemaker, who with Abner departs on detective work
to help clear the name of the hero. The final scene between the
two honest, rough mountaineers movingly shows the clumsy
affection and respect they have for each other. Harben was wise
to revive these popular pillars of the hills.

In the story, Abner purchases the Darley newspaper, *The New
Clarion*, and makes Howard Tinsley the editor. Abner's rural
philosophy and Tinsley's technical knowledge make the paper a
success until on circumstantial evidence Tinsley is accused of
murder. Everyone deserts him except his sweetheart, Mary
Trumbley, who runs the newspaper while he is in jail, and Abner
and Pole, who set out to clear the young man. When they finally
uncover the killer, Tinsley and Mary are free to marry, the
newspaper continues to be a success, and Abner and Pole
become local heroes.

The dialogue is colorfully authentic throughout, and there is a
delightfully comic interlude concerning the banquet given at the
Johnston House for the rural correspondents of the newspaper.
An elaborate meal is served in courses—not a "regular dump-all-

in-a-pile dinner"—beginning with "a fancy soup, boolyon" (111). Although the humor here is realistic and subtle, at times throughout the book, Abner's or Pole's long, extraneous stories interfere with the progress of the plot. One such unnecessary tale is a brief retelling of an early Harben short story, "A Filial Impulse," this time concerning young Abner's return from the West when he hears of his brother's death and his reunion with his mother.

Thanks to the reappearances of Abner Daniel, Pole Baker, and the mountaineers of Darley, *The New Clarion* is a pleasant exception to the list of failures during Harben's last ten years.

VI   The Inner Law

Harben's next novel, *The Inner Law*, 1915, was an ambitious failure. His better works covered a more logical time span than the twenty-five years encompassed in this one. It is divided into four parts, and William Dean Howells's earlier criticism of *Westerfelt* is appropriate here: if Harben had sustained the quality of the first part throughout the other three, he might have produced a substantial American novel. He did not, and the result is another piece of ultra-romantic escapism.

Part I introduces young Carter Crofton, son of an Atlanta millionaire, a promising poet who is looked upon by literary circles as another Sidney Lanier or Edgar Allan Poe. The Crofton family has a history of licentiousness, and, indeed, when Carter visits his uncle in the hills of North Georgia, he seduces Lydia Romley, unschooled daughter of the uncle's housekeeper, and then deserts her to care for his ill father. The elder Crofton soon dies in an asylum in Cincinnati (similar to the death of Harben's father), and Carter leaves the country for a life of glamour in Europe. His seduction of Lydia becomes for him a mere experiment in romance.

Part II briefly describes the twenty-five years of Carter's pursuit of frivolity, vanity, collapsing career in letters, and eventual dissipation, while part III depicts his return to America, a physically deteriorated and spiritually empty man of forty-six. Unable to forget the wronged Lydia, who has become a successful nurse, he is full of remorse and dissatisfaction.

In part IV a decidedly changed Carter lives a simple, Tolstoyan life in New York City, ashamed of his wealth and former luxurious living. He reads the great philosophers and becomes a modest philanthropist, but still unhappy, contemplates suicide often. He befriends Joe "Socrates" Allen, a young man with literary aspirations who lives in a Bohemian colony in New Jersey, and the two develop a close father-son relationship. Even the dullest reader will guess that Joe is Carter's own son, the offspring of his seduction of Lydia. Their friendship and the subsequent accidental meeting of Carter and Lydia are outrageous coincidences; yet Harben withholds the truth until the end. After many emotional turmoils, Carter and Lydia are reconciled and plan to take their son, now a poet with a promising future, to California to devote their lives to him.

The only really believable segment of the book is part I, in which Harben subtly condemns Carter for his shallowness and pretentiousness. When his father dies, Carter is sure the newspapers will emphasize "the son who was bringing home the remains for interment—the brilliant son of whom the State was so proud, and who now had the heartfelt sympathy of the public at large in his great bereavement."[13] The change in Carter is not so subtly depicted. His rebirth in middle age and his search for the meaning of life through idealistic philosophy and through a realization that God's inner law is more uplifting and right than the display of outward pretences give the book its title; but his conversion is too forced and sentimental to be convincing.

The value of the rural life as opposed to the urban is again emphasized; and, as usual, Harben's scenes in the hill country remain his best and most authentic. But there are too few of them in this novel. The Bohemian existence of Joe Allen and his friends is too happy and artificial to be realistic. The whole of part IV, in fact, being bathos from beginning to end, weakens whatever power part I had.

The Inner Law, in the final analysis, emerges as a drawn-out, unsuccessful melodrama. The New York *Times* reported that "there is good stuff in this book";[14] unfortunately, the "bad stuff" counteracts the good.

VII Second Choice

In *Second Choice* (1916), which he dedicated to Robert Loveman, Harben included enough adequate character sketches to make the novel interesting; but the plot line is again too melodramatic to consider it wholly convincing. Even the evil characters, whom the reader comes to despise in the course of the book, repent and become noble persons. The New York *Times* said of the novel, "While realizing Mr. Harben's power and recognizing his standing as a novelist, . . . 'Second Choice' reads like a book written by a formula."[15] The *Literary Digest* used the book to question Harben's excessive popularity, concluding that his inevitable happy endings, false though they may be, form the constant charm.[16]

In part I Wynn Dunham, the hero, is in much the same predicament as Gilbert Neal in Harben's earlier novel of that name. He supports his family on a farm, his father is grateful toward his son, and his mother shows favoritism toward his brother George, a wastrel just released from prison. Wynn loves Edna Wrenn, pathetically weak daughter of Leticia Wrenn, an impoverished but grandiose widow who connives to have Edna marry Virginia blue-blood Morris Stockton. Edna's adolescent sister, Cora, "a little girl with a man's brain,"[17] is fiercely loyal to Wynn. By the end of part I, George has stolen Wynn's life savings, Edna has married Stockton, and Wynn has lost his job with the local cotton mill and has left his unpleasant life for parts unknown.

Part II begins five years later. Wynn, who has become rich in Montana, forgives his brother before George dies in a boarding house in Montana—a scene strikingly similar to reports of the death of Harben's own brother in Texas. Wynn returns to Georgia, invests one hundred thousand dollars in a new cotton mill which he is to run, employs Stockton, whose luck has steadily gone downhill, and marries his second choice, Cora, who has retained her spontaneity and faithfulness to Wynn.

Cora and Mrs. Wrenn emerge as the best-drawn characters. Only fifteen years old in part I, Cora shows unusual spirit, pride, and common sense, much like a younger Dixie Hart. She is able to view her family's situation realistically and in vain urges them to stop living in the dream world of the past:

It makes me sick to hear people talking about blue blood, old names, and such things, in this day of hard struggle for existence. . . . In my opinion, the best people are the ones that make the most out of their opportunities, and the person that refuses to work because his ancestors didn't 'is the most deplorable specimen of dry rot in the world. When people smirk, and grin, and talk to me about who the Wrenns were sixty

years ago, and I have on stockings with holes in them that can't be
darned, and no money nor credit to get new ones, why—well, I'd just as
soon be called Sigglefritz as anything else. (87)

Cora categorizes her mother precisely when she calls her family
"a lot of respectable dead beats; they don't really know it, but
that's what they are" (126). Mrs. Wrenn's false airs and plottings
are endless: "That little widow is the damnedest, sharpest little
woman in seven states. . . . She manages to put a front on her
that sweeps everything out of her track that ain't of use to her"
(112). This scheming mother, a relic of the gentlewoman of the
old South, is completely blind to reality and lives in a world of
illusion.

   Second Choice is another mediocre story by Harben—not good
enough to be considered successful, not bad enough to be
overlooked.

VIII   The Triumph

   Harben regained literary stature with the publication of *The
Triumph* in 1917. This historical novel in three parts is set in
preCivil War days, during the war itself, and in the reconstruction period. Early reviews were mixed. The New York *Times*
called it Harben's best work:

"The Triumph" contains all the tragedy of the great struggle and the
even greater readjustment that followed it; and through all the story
moves the grim, heart-worn, humorous and pathetic figure of Andrew
Merlin—really a decided achievement in character drawing. Mr.
Harben's new novel contains many of the elements that make for real
greatness. On a distinctly American theme, and written by a master of
the surroundings he has chosen to depict, there can be no doubt that
"The Triumph" is a distinctly noteworthy book.[18]

The *Nation*, on the other hand, finding in the book little
justification for William Dean Howells's appreciation of Harben
(reprinted as a preface to *The Triumph*), labelled the work
perfunctory: "Harben has not worked freely or spontaneously,
and his product is too plainly a made affair."[19] More recently,
Robert Bush has maintained that the novel has the power of
great tragedy: "A single commonplace household epitomizes the
suffering of the House Divided on the national scale. The

tragedy is dramatized with dignity and credibility, and over all is not only the power of Merlin's conscience, but his ability to see even beyond the prejudices of his own side."[20]

The plot concerns Andrew Merlin, an honest, sensitive, middleage Georgian, and his family. The chief issue is Andrew's total commitment to his belief in the equality of blacks and whites, a viewpoint which makes him an outsider in the village of Delbridge. Directly opposed to him is his brother, Thomas, the chief slaveholder of the county, whom Harben makes as likable and understanding as his brother.

Part I effectively establishes the situation and thoroughly analyzes the major characters. Ruth, Andrew's wife, is a frail woman who publicly stands by her husband but who inwardly believes he is wrong in his unpopular sentiments; she spoils their son, Bob, who is ashamed of his father. Their daughter Anne, however, supports her father and his notions; there are hints of a budding romance between her and Arthur Preston, son of a proslavery family who lives next door. Andrew's outspoken views and his freeing of a slave left to him in payment of a debt cause him to be ostracized by the community to a point where he is burned in effigy. Shortly after the war breaks out, Andrew escapes a vigilante committee set on killing him or forcing him to join the Confederacy, and joins the Union army.

Part II opens two years later as Andrew, having lost one leg in battle, returns to Delbridge and his family. Bob is still vehemently opposed to his father, Anne remains faithful and consoling, and Ruth, whose sanity has been affected by the events of the war, is relentlessly bitter toward her husband. Bob enlists in the Confederate army to atone for his father's "treason" and is killed; Ruth's mind completely breaks; she dies with no reconciliation with Andrew. When the Ku Klux Klan raids their house, Andrew and Anne are forced to take refuge in the hills of North Carolina for several months.

In part III, "the long struggle drew to an end. The courageous South was beaten and starved into a state of utter helplessness."[21] Thomas Merlin, now a brigadier general, returns to Delbridge a local hero and shuns his estranged brother, who is considered a traitor. However, the brothers are reunited when Thomas courageously and successfully defends Andrew against a Klan mob. In a move somewhat out of character, Andrew shrewdly makes a profit on the sale of land to Yankee investors, while

Anne and Arthur, also a Confederate hero, plan to marry.
Andrew "had lost his wife, with whom he had hoped to spend his
last years. He had lost his son who he had thought would take his
place and keep his name alive; and now, in a certain sense, he
was losing his daughter" (396). But he had remained true to his
ideals and convictions, so "infinite peace descended upon him.
. . . He had won. In life's grim battle the triumph was his" (397).
  The Triumph is one of Harben's strongest statements on the
issue of equal rights. Although he again showed an understanding
for the feelings of Southerners who supported slavery and
segregation, Andrew Merlin's convictions and beliefs, by far the
most convincing and best developed in the book, represent
Harben's own: "The long and short of it is that the Lord God
Almighty has planted in the breasts o' *some* folks the idea that
every human being is entitled to an equal chance to live out his
days on earth, and slave-ownin' will have to go, for you know,
and I know, that yore wife's niggers hain't got the same chance in
the pursuit of happiness as yore sons" (18). Joe, the slave Andrew
set free, becomes a spokesman for his disoriented race after the
war, speaking at public gatherings of displaced slaves who are
unaccustomed to their new-found freedom:

What y'-all got ter do . . . is ter put yo' flat foot down on yo' legal rights
en stan' fer um ef de sky fall on yer lak er load er bricks f'um er
dumpcart. Dis big government done set you free wid its blood, en it's
gwine ter see to it dat yer gits yo' rights. Y'-all is 'fraid er de Kuklux, en
I don't blame yer much, fer ef dar is anything dat is calculate' ter make
de blood of a cullud man run cold it is dem white ghosts wid caps on, en
hangin'-ropes in deir clutch. But yer must put up wid dem, too, ef you
gwine stan' fer yo' rights, as new, free men. (338)

  But more important than the racial issue *per se* is Andrew
Merlin's commitment to his own integrity in his search for what is
right. Except for Anne, he is isolated from his family and
neighbors, even though "since time begun the man that did
plumb right has been scoffed at and ridiculed by others" (119).
Andrew has obeyed the voice of his conscience throughout his
life and justifies his independent stand when he states, "It seems
to me that whatever a human bein' wants to do, that has courage
in it, it is right in God's sight" (230). In 1913 Harben had written
an article for the *Bookman* in which he confirmed the fact that
he intended a universal as well as a regional application of his

works: "I am asking myself what has any writer in any land found
to write about which may not be found in Georgia—granting, of
course, the premise that the heart and soul of man is vitally the
same the world over, and that these are the only things really
worth writing about."[22] Andrew's predicament is a choice
application of this principle, for his experience is the experience
of the national conscience from the prewar years into the
reconstruction period. In fact, the alienation of the Merlin
brothers could symbolize the animosity between North and
South. Their final reconciliation is meaningful on the national
level as the symbol of genuine reunion between North and
South.[23] "I used to think the Lord favored the right side in the
war, but I don't think so now. It seems to me that he loves both
sides alike in this present mix-up. It's just his children a-fussin'
over a trifle, an' he wants 'em to quiet down" (222).

Harben held much the same attitude Samuel L. Clemens held
concerning the South's eagerness for the war: too many
Southerners saw only the romantic glamour of it and foolishly
ignored the brutal reality it would mean:

Around Delbridge, all through the mountains, a new sort of activity was
rife. . . . Men too old for service and boys too young were bubbling
over with the spirit of fresh, indignant adventure. Most of them were
born for the saddle and the chase. Deer and bear were becoming
extinct in the mountains; the Indians had moved away; here was a new
thing to kill—a beast of invasion that dared to dictate the changes to be
made in their laws. (156)

The trials of the civilian Southerners during the war are
depicted powerfully, and the postwar rehabilitation of
Delbridge is told just as masterfully. Harben, trying to find some
balance to its existence, makes the village a microcosm of the
South.

Harben drew upon his own family's history, three short stories,
and a novel for parts of *The Triumph*. His own father might well
have been the model for Andrew Merlin, for the elder Harben
was as self-reliant and firm in his convictions as the fictional
character. The Harben family, like the Merlin family, took
refuge in the hills of North Carolina during the war. Harben's
sisters' husbands fought on opposite sides during the war, as
Andrew and Thomas in the novel do. "The Sale of Uncle
Rastus" was incorporated in a brief episode in which Thomas is

being forced to sell his favorite slaves, Rastus and Sambo, until the intervention of his alienated brother. Harben combined "The Whipping of Uncle Henry" and "A Humble Abolitionist" in the more fully developed dilemma of Andrew and his slave, Joe. When Joe refuses to work, Andrew sets out to whip him until the slave obliquely threatens him, as Uncle Henry had gently threatened Jasper Pelham. Later Andrew frees Joe over the objections of the community, as the Gills had done in the earlier story. Andrew outwits the Yankee investors in the same manner the elder Bishop had done in *Abner Daniel.* Although Harben had already begun to take bits of plot from his early works, he does so effectively and naturally in this novel.

The Triumph is a powerful, well told novel of epic proportions, one of Harben's very best. He is seldom overly sentimental, there are no absurd coincidences, every character is as well drawn as any he had ever handled, he is subdued in his rhetoric. On the whole, the novel is believable, subtle, and moving.

IX   The Hills of Refuge

In an interview with Joyce Kilmer in 1917, Harben deplored the state of the novel of his day, stating that the genre was doomed because contemporary novelists were too unrealistic and pretentious to capture the interests of the reading public successfully.[24] His theory may well be applied to his own 1918 novel, *The Hills of Refuge.* In it Harben regressed to his Virginia Demarest style and produced a thirdrate romance with no redeeming qualities. The plot concerns Bostonian Charles Browne, who takes the blame for his brother's embezzlement at a bank and begins a new life as a farmhand for a family in Georgia. He aids the family physically, morally, and financially, and eventually marries the daughter.

Harben's writing here is atrocious: the style is hurried and juvenile, the characters are wooden and stereotypical, the dialogue is artificial and cheap, the situations are contrived and absurd. *The Hills of Refuge* is as hackneyed as a motion picture melodrama, which indeed it became.[25] It is inferior in all respects, and is especially disappointing coming directly after Harben's fine work in *The Triumph.*

X   *Harben's Last Years*

During his last ten years Harben was still a striking figure. He was slim, with clearcut features, piercing brown eyes, white hair and mustache. "I remember Uncle Will well in New York. He was 6 feet 7 inches tall, interested in every person and loved by children."[26] He was a member of the Authors' Club, which met every Saturday afternoon in a studio in Carnegie Hall, and of the National Institute of Arts and Letters.[27]

Although Harben had had pleasant associations with prominent literary figures of the day, for the most part he began to shun such company, preferring instead to live with the kind of people he wrote about:

> I resolved a long time ago to try to avoid living with literary people and to live with all sorts of human beings—with people who didn't know or care whether or not I was a writer.
>
> So I have for my friends and acquaintances sailors, merchants—people of all sorts of professions and trades. And people of that sort—people who make no pretentions to be artists—are the best company for a writer, for they open their hearts to him. A writer can learn how to write about humanity by living with humanity, instead of with other people who are trying to write about humanity.[28]

His favorite gathering place was a shack which had been a tool shed in an undeveloped section of Riverside Drive Park. His regular companions included a mystic, a Chinese scholar, several artists, a Catholic Irishman, a journalist, and any other loiterer—schooled or unschooled—who cared to join them. This company, which loved the outdoors and the smell of burning, water soaked logs, often lunched there, roasting potatoes in the coals and making pots of black coffee. They expressed their thoughts freely on any topic—life, death, religion, art, literature, government.[29] As the leader of the group, Harben "was the brother to all men and made them free of heart. . . . Had it not been for his family he would have given his entire substance to his fellow man, with no thought except that it was the obvious thing to do. His was a Tolstoyan sort of feeling toward the world."[30] Soon the curious crowds grew so large that the park department had to forbid further use of the shack as the meeting place for the group.[31]

According to a grandson, in his meanderings in the park Harben usually dressed like "an old derelict." He made friends with a young woman who sketched there, and they chatted daily; he spoke to her of his son, which she thought "a bit of persiflage on the old bum's part." To her astonishment, one day Harben came to the park "dressed to kill, with a six-foot, four-inch sailor with eyes like ship's lanterns." The result of this meeting was that the sailor (Harben's son Chandler) and the young lady were married.[32] That Harben retained his wit and sense of humor during these years is evidenced by the Machiavellian joke he played on the family of his new daughter-in-law. He gave them a full-bound set of his books sometime after the marriage. Fifteen years later, long after Harben's death, one of his grandsons came upon them and asked his maternal grandfather what they were. "Oh, some set of books that your grandfather gave us years ago" was the reply, his tone suggesting that books from an author was a cheap gift, the sort of thing one might expect from that odd crowd. The grandson opened the books and found to his astonishment—and the maternal grandfather's—that they were publisher's dummies; all the pages were blank. The grandson concluded, "That's a rather remarkable way to get a last laugh. The Werners were *not* readers. But could W. N. H. have known that they would never crack *one* of those books over all those long years? This was fully twelve years after his death."[33]

During World War I Harben used his knowledge of farming and was instrumental in planting a community-wide victory garden in New York, utilizing a large vacant lot opposite his apartment. Two Columbia University professors, an artist, an Englishman, Harben, and several others planted corn, beans, and tomatoes in an effort to conserve food, while their wives knitted sweaters, socks, and mufflers for the soldiers. The garden was a means to pleasant camaraderie as much as anything else, but it soon became so famous locally that a New York newspaper reporter interviewed Harben for a story about it and took pictures of him in the war garden.[34]

During the summer of 1919, Harben's health began to fail. He vacationed at the seashore, thinking the sea air would improve him; instead, since he did not bother about consulting a doctor,

he was worse when he returned to New York. After a brief
illness, he died of intestinal problems at his home on August 7,
1919, at the age of sixty-one. His daughter, Elizabeth, was six at
the time: "All I remember is that I saw him, lying dead in bed,
while I was peeking through a glass door that had a sheer type
curtain covering each of the double doors. He was so interested
in the world beyond the living one that Mother said he was
ready to go on to see what was on the other side."[35] Harben's
body was taken to Dalton and interred in the West Hill
Cemetery on August 11, 1919. His obituary in the New York
Times accurately noted that "in his writings he remained faithful
to the surroundings of his youth."[36] He left two unpublished
novels, which appeared within the next year.

XI   The Cottage of Delight

The first posthumous novel, *The Cottage of Delight,* was
published in 1919, shortly after Harben's death. The setting is
Ridgeville, a mill town in Northern Georgia where John Trott, a
contractor's assistant, lives with his mother, Lizzie, a prostitute
and heavy drinker. Though agnostic in his beliefs, John is a
morally decent sort, despite the immoral behavior of his mother.
He supervises the building of a court house in a Tennessee
village and falls in love with Tilly Whaley, daughter of a
narrowminded conservative who objects to John's agnostic bent.
Despite Whaley's disapproval, John marries Tilly and takes her
back to Ridgeville to their "cottage of delight."

When Whaley eventually discovers that John's mother is a
fallen woman, Tilly, to prevent him from killing John, returns to
Tennessee with her father, leaving a note of explanation which
John never receives. Thinking his bride has deserted him, John
leaves his unhappy life in Ridgeville. His train derails in a
spectacular railroad tragedy, but he escapes injury and settles in
New York. He is presumed dead by everyone in Ridgeville,
where his mother suddenly relinquishes her sinful life and
becomes a pious woman.

Part II opens ten years later. John has prospered in New York,
and in Ridgeville Tilly has married a former suitor, Joel Eperson,
and the couple has two children. She has befriended Lizzie
Trott, who is now "Grandmother Trott" to the children. John
impulsively returns, provides for his mother, and declares his

love for Tilly, who will not desert her husband. The book ends with John preparing to return to a lonely life in New York, and with Tilly determined to endure an unhappy life without him. But on the last page, Harben supplies the inevitable happy ending for the lovers by suggesting that Joel, who sees himself as a complete failure in life, will kill himself so the lovers can be reunited: "After all, there is one thing that I can do for him that he could not do for me."[37]

Because the book is sporadically interesting, it is understandable how a motion picture could be made of it:[38] it spans years, is romantic and melodramatic, and contains the contrast of exciting and tranquil scenes. The first section, concerning John and his situation in Ridgeville, is realistic and powerful; but once romance enters the picture, the situation becomes histrionic, and the usual coincidences and exaggerations occur. John's self-sacrificing instinct blights the story with excessive sentiment, while Lizzie's overnight conversion is forced and unconvincing.

Religious bigotry is again one of Harben's themes. John is the self-reliant hero who will not pretend to embrace a faith he cannot believe in; but, like George Dawson in *Jane Dawson*, he does not interfere with Tilly's faith. The fanatical views of Tilly's father are an exaggeration of the fundamentalism of the rural community; his dilemma is having a son-in-law who is an extreme agnostic and the son of a prostitute.[39] But compared to *Jane Dawson*, the handling of the religious angle here is listless and outworn.

The Cottage of Delight was one of Harben's personal favorites, and though it has a newness in the early part, it also embodies many of his commonplace and overused ideas. The book is another example of his failure to sustain the promising mood of his earlier chapters. While not a complete failure, *The Cottage of Delight* is, in the long run, less than adequate.

XII   The Divine Event

Harben's final novel was *The Divine Event*, written several years before he died, but not published until 1920. Since the death of his son Eric in 1911, Harben had been intrigued with the continuation of life after death. In a letter to a fellow novelist, he complimented the writer on a recent book: "It is the sort of thing . . . that I believe in. It strikes me that you are

something of a mystic—I hope so, I am sure, for the mystics are
the only writers who produce living matter."[40] Unfortunately,
Harben was not enough of a mystic himself, for *The Divine Event*
is one of his inferior works.

Immortality is a theme of this novel, where one of the main
characters is the spirit of a dead person. Before his death,
millionaire Morten Gramling became obsessed with mysticism
and immortality. Since his death, his brother Hillery has had
mysterious psychic experiences. Hillery enlists the aid of
Professor Trimble, an expert in psychic phenomena, and the two
men communicate with Morten. From the grave Morten assures
Hillery of the beauty of the afterlife, and instructs him to leave
his fine life and live with the poor in New York. Hillery moves to
the East Side and is attracted to a young woman of mystery,
Lucia Lingle. Neither knows the true circumstances of the other;
and though she does not know who he is, Morten comes from
beyond the grave to advise Lucia several times.

Lucia finally admits that she is an heiress whose half-brother
had already murdered her brother and had her declared insane
so he would inherit her fortune. Through the use of psychic
phenomena, Hillery and Professor Trimble thwart the half-
brother, and Hillery and Lucia begin a life together. Morten and
his new friend, Lucia's dead brother, literally ride off into the
horizon together, supposedly leaving the reader with the
assurance of an afterlife.

Harben began the novel with explanations for and questions
about mystic experiences, but soon reverted to a routine
detective story. Hillery and Professor Trimble become lay
facsimiles of Minard Hendricks and Dr. Lampton of Harben's
earlier detective novels, with the accent shifting to their
defeating the villainous half-brother. The subject of mysticism
becomes subordinate—perhaps fortunately—for the novel is
amateurishly written.

Harben handles aristocratic characters more smoothly and
naturally than in previous attempts, but not so successfully as his
mountain characters, none of whom appear in this novel. He does
realistically describe some of the deplorable working conditions
of the day in sweatshops, where "people grind in reeking
dungeons," but in portraying the conditions of the poor uses
bathos rather than pathos, compounding the misfortune of the
poverty stricken with trite, tactless dialogue: "Her father's lying

in the kitchen now—he's full of booze for a week. We are out of food. He sold my shoes that was given to me."[41]

The Divine Event was an unhappy ending to Harben's thirty-year literary career. This last decade of his life had produced many of his worst novels, one of his finest, and several mediocre ones.

CHAPTER 6

Final Analysis

ALTHOUGH Harben was one of the most popular and prolific writers of his own day, he has since sunk into relative oblivion. His novels are now out of print, his stories are rarely anthologized, and he is seldom mentioned even in listings of writers of his era. Changing public taste accounts for part of this obscurity, and much of his writing—decidedly erratic—does not satisfy the critical criteria for lasting literature. With thirty novels and numerous short stories, Harben wrote too much. Had he written less and perfected what he did write, he might have found a place in the front ranks of American literature. Unfortunately for readers today, he chose the route of momentary, popular success.

But perhaps such neglect is unwarranted. Harben's honesty and sincerity in depicting the people and customs of his own North Georgia region enabled him to make a distinct contribution, however minor, to American literature. His quiet, rich treatment of this secluded area demonstrates his power of glorifying the commonplace; despite his flaws, he deserves to be recognized.

I   *Realism Versus Romanticism*

During the 1890s and the first two decades of the twentieth century, the thirty years which comprised Harben's writing career, Realism and Romanticism were both expressions of the time—one dealing with the actuality of the present and the other with nostalgia for the past. As a regional writer Harben found it difficult to make a distinction between his own leanings toward Realism and the public's taste for Romanticism. He had a strong urge to write realistically of life in North Georgia as he knew it

firsthand; but mixed with this interest was the need to satisfy
readers' cravings for conventional love stories and characters.
Such contradiction of purpose led to a curious mixture of Realism
and Romanticism in all his works.

On one hand, his typical heroes are always stereotypically
noble, while his standard heroines are beautiful women oozing
with Victorian virtue—the sort of gentility popular audiences
demanded. His plots are often of a hackneyed sameness: a wrong
to be righted, a misunderstanding to be reconciled, a conversion
from bad to good. But in his depictions of the North Georgia
mountaineers, he revealed the normal, unglamorous side of the
common lives of these hill people: their grievances, joys,
prejudices, traditions, and superstitions. At times the blight of
sentimentality is on them as well, but for the most part Harben
viewed his mountaineers honestly, as human beings with
universal feelings and emotions, not as mere symbols of economic
wrong or of idealistic retreat. This combination of Realism and
Romanticism makes Harben a product of his confused age, and
suggests why none of his books may be consistently categorized:
his predominantly Realistic novels are marred, however slightly,
by antiquated effusiveness, and his sentimental romances often
include realistic scenes which are incongruous with the intended
romance.

An argument between William Dean Howells and Samuel L.
Clemens concerning Harben illustrates this ambiguity of the age.
Shortly before Clemens's death Howells had recommended
Harben to him highly. Clemens could not deny the honesty of
Harben's works, but he angrily wrote Howells that he disliked
the Georgian for focusing on sordid and ugly conditions. Howells
noted, "At heart Clemens was romantic, and he would have had
the world of fiction stately and handsome and whatever the real
world was not."[1] Howells's reply to Clemens was defensive,
though mild, since he would not unduly upset the dying man:

I have not a Fairy Princess to take my profane and abusive dictation,
and so I cannot reply to your praises of our favorite author in fit terms,
but you will find my joy in Harben in an early number of the *N.
American*. You seem to require a novelist to be true to the facts and if
the facts are not pleasant, to be pleasant himself. That seems rather
difficult. You are the only man who can do it; but I believe you will end
by liking poor old Harben as much as I do. He didn't make north
Georgia; he only made a likeness of it. Don't shoot the artist.[2]

Howells implied that Clemens was as uncertain of his aims as Harben was; when romance confronted reality, Clemens opted for romance—or at least reality glossed over with romance. Clemens would have preferred a more pleasant view of life in Harben's works; Howells appreciated Harben's adherence to the commonplace. Harben combined both qualities.

In a rather overwrought manner, Harben's sister Kate went further than Clemens in denouncing her brother. She accused him of prostituting himself, of selling himself to an age which, in her opinion, demanded primarily the ugly facts instead of the "omnipresent potential good which is the supreme value of Creative Art."[3] Because she preferred the genteel view of life, she insisted that his realistic bent was a destructive influence in his writings.

Harben considered himself more a Realist than a Romanticist, but with a difference: "The trouble with the average realist . . . is that he doesn't believe that the emotions are real. As a matter of fact, the greatest source of material for a novelist is to be found in the emotional and spiritual side of human nature. If writers were more receptive to spiritual and emotional impressions they would make better novels."[4] Too often, however, Harben tempered his Realism with idealized rather than genuine emotion, with the result being oppressive sentimentality which detracted from the reality of his works. His depiction of the emotions of his aristocratic characters, for example, is false and unconvincing because such untrue emotions are forced. He presented few, if any, patrician characters successfully, for theirs was an artificial world which Harben never completely understood. But this was not the case with his own primitive countrymen of North Georgia. He saw the happiness and the pathos of their rude lives and convincingly portrayed their humor, their unsophisticated religious beliefs, their independence from rules, their proud sensitivity, and their stoic isolation. Howells appreciated Harben's depiction of the emotions of the hill folk: "The passions are lords among these primitive people: avarice, envy, hate, revenge, lust, ambition, rule the men of Mr. Harben's mountaineers."[5]

Whenever Harben's aristocratic world comes in contact with his mountain world, the distinction between the two life styles is made much more obvious. Harben commented on this contrast himself, at the same time characterizing his mountaineers precisely:

Maeterlinck says somewhere that we go about with great thoughts and vast yearnings in our souls, seldom daring to open our hearts to our neighbours. I think this is especially true of town and city life. A man in an evening suit studying a wine-list is not so likely to tell you all about his wife's infidelity as a hod-carrier in mud-stained overalls would be. So I think that I got nearer to the heart of humanity by knowing the crude, frank types in the mountains of Georgia than I could by daily intercourse with the most talkative denizens of any metropolis. . . . The man of town conventions will stare at the cold face of his dead daughter and make stereotyped replies to wooden sympathies, while the mountain farmer will sob as he leans on a rail fence of his cabin and tell a full-faced group all about the child he has lost, or he may mutely stagger away quite as eloquently under the drab duties of his life. . . .

The metropolitan when he learns that his daughter has disgraced him hides his shame behind his morning paper and consults his lawyer, while the mountaineer takes down his gun from its rack and stalks forth to kill as regardless of consequences as the most primitive man. And what he says to sympathetic friends whom he meets on the way, and what they say to him along with their looks and actions would make undying literature. How can an observant writer fail to find material among such individuals, and amid such scenes?[6]

II *Local Color with a Difference*

Harben indeed made use of such firsthand experiences. He believed, as did Howells, that a national literature could best be built by writers picturing faithfully the material with which they are most familiar. His own role was to leave a series of works which would accurately depict phases of life in his North Georgia mountains. Like the best local colorists, Harben exploited the peculiarities of his region to entertain readers from all sections of the country; his work is noteworthy for its accurate use of dialect, its authentic presentation of character types, and its careful descriptions of a particular way of life. Howells complimented Harben on his accomplishments in local color: "Of all our localists, as I may call the type of American writers whom I think the most national, no one has done things more expressive of the life he was born to than Mr. Harben."[7] Despite his leanings toward sentimentality, which was common to most local colorists, Harben successfully caught the atmosphere of his section; he had a remarkable understanding of the intricacies of North Georgia life.

In some local-color writing, the locality is sometimes difficult to see for the color: numerous overplayed expressions and misspelled jargon spill from the pages of some writers who attempt to capture native dialects. Harben's dialects, though overdone at the beginning of his career, were on the whole sensitively just reproductions, because he knew his people intimately: "These mountain types express themselves in a musical parlance which contains interesting vestiges of old English, Scotch and Irish phraseology, and no other form of expression could be better suited to their thoughts and needs. Their speech bubbles with fun and ridicule, and a profanity that is often uttered in a spirit so righteous that it disarms criticism."[8] Both his mountaineer and black dialects are crude, but natural and not overly exaggerated. Although these genuine Southern accents elude all spelling, Harben comes strikingly close to reproducing them; the dialects even today approximate the speech of some North Georgia inhabitants. Howells took special notice of Harben's use of language: "His people talk as if they had not been in books before, and they talk all the more interestingly because they have for the most part not been 'in society,' or ever will be. They express themselves, without straining for dialect, in the neighborly parlance which their experience and their observation have not transcended, and they express themselves with a fury of fun, of pathos and profanity which is native to their region."[9]

Unlike many regional writers of his time, Harben wrote in retrospect, not while he actually lived among the people of his region. After absorbing the atmosphere in Georgia, he left to collect his ideas and set them down. He was at the same time inside and outside the culture about which he wrote, committed to its values, yet capable of achieving a certain detachment:

It sometimes happens that an author can write about the scenes he knows best only after he has gone away from them. I know this is true of myself.

It's in line with the old saws about "distance lends enchantment" and "emotion remembered in tranquillity," you know. I believe that DuMaurier was able to write his vivid descriptions of life in the Latin Quarter of Paris because he went to London to do it.

You see, I absorbed life in Georgia for many years. And in New York I can remember it and get a perspective on it and write about it. . . .

Once I tried to write a novel in Dalton, and I simply couldn't do it.[10]

The memory of a single scene often encouraged a beginning for him, and other recollections swept a story onward. Harben's best characters—Abner Daniel, Pole Baker, Ann Boyd, and Dixie Hart, in the novels of those same names—illustrate this use of personal experience. In the case of each of these novels, Harben first met the real-life people before creating their fictional counterparts and building his plot around them, thereby complementing both plots and characters with the unique qualities of the region.

The fact that most of his characters were based on real people suggests Harben's chief divergence from local colorists. Most local-color writing is an attempt to capture a quaint and charming world before such a world vanishes forever. Harben went beyond merely exploiting pecularities of his region; he was both a historian and a reporter of North Georgia, dedicated to depicting the very change and standardization that local colorists often avoid. His local color assumed a truer tone. He treated his rural people seriously, seeing them as more than pleasant stereotypes of an oldfashioned culture. He never ridiculed them, for he saw the self-reliant qualities beneath their rough exteriors that would eventually become the middle-class ideal of the New South. He did not write about the Jeeter Lesters of Georgia—the hopeless, poverty stricken farmers who lived in squalor and lacked the ambition to liberate themselves from their misery. The lowly and unlearned farmers and villagers Harben portrayed were honorable, persevering, and worthy of the achievement which would result from their earnest work. In Harben's eyes the moral character and social rise of such mountaineers represented an optimistic prophecy of the democracy of the South.[11] For example, Alan and Adele Bishop, the younger generation in *Abner Daniel*, have already discarded the careless dialect of their parents and have broadened their cultural horizons. The innate shrewdness and executive ability of Pole Baker would eventually blossom in his descendants. Gilbert and Dave Neal are dissatisfied with their poverty; since they are equipped with the necessary ambition and drive to better themselves economically and socially, both achieve success, though in different ways. Harben himself maintained, "From such stock Georgia is getting her best lawyers, best all-round citizens and richest men. Ambition seems to have been asleep and wakened afresh; descendants of leaders are becoming leaders again."[12]

Harben, who in fact traced the origin of many of his mountaineers, discovered that they were of English descent. Their names and customs were strongly reminiscent of English country life, while their legends and their ancestors, so far as they could be traced, led directly back to Virginia. Apparently they were the descendants of the Virginia colonists who pushed across the frontiers and found new homes in the hills of North Georgia.[13] Their pioneer spirit, their initiative, and their inborn capabilities would eventually produce equally enterprising descendants who would rise to higher levels. Harben's Georgians mirror the determination of the American middle class; they are not merely colorful hill people in romantic vignettes.

III   *The Mountaineers*

The Georgians loved Harben for his accurate depictions of them, and spoke to him freely on every subject. "The mountain Georgians are the most unmasked individuals I ever met. . . . They really make story-telling easier for a writer, for they are story-tellers themselves."[14] He was thoroughly fascinated with these mountaineers. He once stated that he would continue to write about North Georgia for his own satisfaction, whether the public read his works or not:

I get more and more out of it . . . the further I go. And the deeper I go into the lives of these simple people the more I find to wonder at and admire and the deeper I want to go. It is an absorbing study, and my thoughts are so bound up in it that my life is passed not so much in New York as in North Georgia. You have no idea of the depth of emotion of which these people are capable. You might know them a long time and never guess at the passion slumbering deep down in their souls until some chance occasion revealed to you the storm of feeling that had been sleeping concealed from all the world.

They are a taciturn people, little given to demonstration, making light alike of their sufferings and their pleasures, but feeling with the full force of an ardent Southern temperament all the time. And their pride, especially their family pride—it is astounding.[15]

In practically all of his works on these hill people, Harben emphasized the pride they took in their fundamentalist religion. The prevailing religious influence was Methodist or Baptist, and

frequent church services (where men and women sat on opposite
sides of the aisles), revivals, and camp meetings played a
significant part in their lives. One who did not hold steadfast to
the accepted orthodoxy of the community was considered a lost
soul. Harben had been brought up in such an atmosphere
himself, and he quickly rebelled against such strict beliefs. His
own eventual resolution was Unitarianism, a religion of reason.
But traditional religion was so ingrained in him that he could not
rid himself of it, and so many of his novels deal with his search for
a faith he could find comfort in. His spokesmen include Stanley
Clayton (*Almost Persuaded*), Abner Daniel, and George Dawson
(*Jane Dawson*). In his literary arguments with the narrow minded
dogmatism of some of the mountaineers who pronounced
themselves the favored people of God, Harben did not hesitate
to show the country preacher, considered an authority not to be
disputed, to be "sometimes brutal, cruel, in his fanaticism, and
sometimes coarse even to the verge of indecency."[16] But he
never degraded any person who found genuine solace in the
simple faith of the hills.

The church meetings of the mountaineers served the dual
purpose of soul saving and socializing, for these people were
good humored and jovial as well as industrious. Their all-day
camp meetings on Sundays were times for merry making,
picnicking, and courting, as were the corn-shuckings, water-
melon-cuttings, and square dances. In the more sophisticated
village of Darley, the Johnston House was often aglow with the
lights of dances and parties. Both the townspeople and the
farmers of the adjacent countryside loved a good time. Harben
records, "A keen sense of humor is one of their chief
characteristics. . . . It is the shrewd humor in these characters
that make them so lovable. A group of North Georgians never
comes together without this trait becoming apparent. Their
conversations overflow with a canny mirth that is irresistible."[17]

Opposed to this mirth was a characteristic common to
Harben's mountain people, which illustrates their intense pride:
their isolation from or their rebellion against the fixed ideas of a
community, whether such ideas were stubborn social ones or
narrow religious ones. Like Nathaniel Hawthorne's characters,
they are sometimes lonely figures, almost antiheroes, who find it
difficult to feel a kinship with the natural brotherhood of
mankind. Yet they bear their suffering with nobility, courage,
and even trust. Ann Boyd and Jane Dawson are ostracized for

youthful sexual indiscretions. Stanley Clayton and Abner Daniel are outsiders because they speak out against traditional religious orthodoxy. Andrew Merlin *(The Triumph)* and Carson Dwight *(Mam' Linda)* are shunned because of political beliefs; both are unpopular champions of rights for blacks. Yet each character retains his pride and poise, with an individualism that sets him above the characters who conform to outdated values.

IV   *The Racial Dilemma*

An important segment of the North Georgia mountaineers was its black population. Following the Civil War, Southern writers could hardly avoid having strong sectional feelings about the race situation. Harben was aware of the many problems presented by emancipation, and his attitude toward the black was interesting. He was progressive enough to see that slavery had been evil and that the continued Southern mistreatment of the freed black was no less an evil. Yet at the same time he sentimentally depicted blacks as oldfashioned "darkies"; he frequently glorified the "uncles" and "mammies" who remained loyal to their old masters, despite their newly acquired freedom. He always bestowed upon his black characters respect and dignity; but early in his career he succumbed to public taste by thrusting upon them a full repertory of shuffles, eye-rollings, and servile gestures. Until 1907 Harben vacillated in his feelings about equal rights, undoubtedly afraid of censure from Southern friends. The turning point in his racial attitudes came with the publication of *Mam' Linda,* in which he vigorously committed himself to the side of equal rights. From that time, he never strayed from this position in those books which dealt with the theme of racial interaction, even though some Southerners considered him a traitor to the South because of his sympathetic views toward the black man. This final commitment made him a courageous product of the new South, a South which looked beyond strictly regional concerns.

V   *Harben's Final Place*

Harben had his own unique style and themes, but at the same time his writings can be viewed as an amalgamation of unrelated qualities drawn from many American writers up to his time. His style is as robust and clumsy as that of James Fenimore Cooper,

though his literary offenses are not as numerous as Samuel
Clemens claimed Cooper's to have been. His excessive sentimentality is reminiscent of Theodore Dreiser's style at its worst. His
short stories lack the unity and form that Edgar Allan Poe
advocated; they are closer to the loosely structured tales and
sketches of Washington Irving. But his detective stories are
almost replicas of Poe's tales of ratiocination. His most memorable characters are those who for one reason or another are
isolated from their community—like the main characters in
Nathaniel Hawthorne's stories; Harben, too, emphasized the
effect rather than the cause of such isolation. Though he is not so
deft in his conception and execution of plot as Henry James is, he
is as intensely true to the psychology of his characters as James is
to his. He echoes Ralph Waldo Emerson and Henry David
Thoreau in his ideas on individuality and the redeeming qualities
of nature. Harben's sense of democracy and optimism, of
equalizing social ranks in the aspiring South, brings to mind the
thoughts of Walt Whitman. His droll humor is as effective as
Clemens's and his early attitude and final position concerning
blacks are much the same as Clemens's had been. The religious
problems that surface in Harben's works are the same that
plagued Edwin Arlington Robinson and, later, T. S. Eliot. His
straightforward descriptions of his native region place him
among the local-color writers of his era. Finally, his emphasis on
the commonplace taps the same source as William Dean
Howells's brand of Realism. Although the influence of each of
these writers was probably unconscious and frequently nebulous,
and although Harben did not bring his work to the artistic
completion that each of these writers did, many of their traits are
at least mirrored in his writing.

   In view of his reflections of literary taste in the America of his
era, his use of a quiet Realism, and his authentic and prophetic
treatment of his North Georgia mountains and their people,
Harben deserves more acknowledgment than he presently
receives. Howells accurately observed that Harben's "corner of
that strange 'new South' . . . is alive with what we feel to be
genuine interests and real emotions."[18] Although he could never
be considered a major American author, the passage of time and
further investigation into his works may result in increased
interest in Harben. His place in American literature is that of an
honest and sincere interpreter of rural life in the South.

Notes and References

In the writing of this book, it has been necessary to rely on unpublished (or published and unidentified) materials concerning Harben. For the locations of these materials, the reader is referred to the list of manuscript collections, section three in the Selected Bibliography, especially to Harben's own scrapbook collection, belonging to his daughter, Mrs. Elizabeth Harben Cox; this personal collection is cited throughout as "scrapbook clipping."

Chapter One

1. "Compliments Dalton and the Argus," Dalton *Argus,* n.d., scrapbook clipping.
2. Katherine Harben Jones, "Life and the Girl," first volume of unpublished memoirs of Harben's youngest sister, belonging to Mrs. Aileen F. Alley, Dalton, Georgia, pp. 159-60. Harben's pride in his impressive lineage became obvious in many of his novels, in which the breeding and social standing of his heroes and heroines are often a determining factor in their romantic relationships; the perfect match had each party of equal social standing.
3. The dedication of *The Caruthers Affair* reads: "To Sir Henry and Lady Harben in warmest memory of the beauty and good cheer at Warnham Lodge."
4. Jones, "Life and the Girl," p. 43.
5. *Ibid.,* p. 48. Harben used this autobiographical information to advantage in a later novel. In fact, there are many parallels between his life and his works. Such autobiographical aspects will be pointed out as the works are discussed.
6. *Ibid.,* p. 75.
7. *Ibid.,* p. 157.
8. *Ibid.,* p. 36.
9. *Ibid.,* p. 124.
10. Rose B. Johnson, "Will N. Harben, Georgia Novelist," M.A. Thesis, University of Georgia, 1925, p. 3. Miss Johnson obtained this information from one of Harben's boyhood friends.
11. Lillian Foster, "Editorial: Will N. Harben," n.p.: n.d., scrapbook clipping. Miss Foster's article seems to have been syndicated to newspapers sometime in 1893.

12. *Ibid.*

13. "Harben's Heart Was in Dixie," Richmond *Evening Journal*, August 19, 1919, p. 6.

14. Foster, "Editorial: Will N. Harben," scrapbook clipping.

15. Jones, "Life and the Girl," p. 118.

16. *Ibid.*, pp. 121, 136.

17. Katherine Harben Jones, "The Girl in the Universe," second volume of unpublished memoirs of Harben's youngest sister, belonging to Mrs. Aileen F. Alley, Dalton, Georgia, pp. 390-91.

18. *Ibid.*, p. 96.

19. Jones, "Life and the Girl," p. 123.

20. *Ibid.*, pp. 122-23.

21. *Ibid.*, pp. 126-27.

22. *Ibid.*, pp. 127-28.

23. *Ibid.*, p. 8.

24. *Ibid.*, p. 124, and Jones, "The Girl in the Universe," p. 315.

25. Jones, "Life and the Girl," pp. 137-38.

26. Vivian M. Moses, "Why Will N. Harben Found in That Country and Its People Interesting Material for His Story-Building," New York *Times*, August 13, 1905, Sec. 3, p. 3.

27. Johnson, "Will N. Harben," p. 5. The country store became an important fixture in practically every novel Harben wrote about his mountaineer friends; in several stories he even used his own habit of avoiding customers.

28. W. Trox Bankston, "A Literary Crown," *North Georgia Citizen*, Dalton, Georgia, n.d., scrapbook clipping.

29. Johnson, "Will N. Harben," pp. 3-4.

30. Jones, "The Girl in the Universe," p. 257.

31. Johnson, "Will N. Harben," pp. 5-6; one of the former "little girls" told Miss Johnson this story in a letter.

32. Jones, "The Girl in the Universe," pp. 300-01.

33. *Ibid.*, pp. 301-11.

34. Kate stated that "Will says Robert can write verses, good ones! Will Harben doesn't care a bit if the Lovemans are Jews, and he likes Robert better than any boy in town"; "The Girl in the Universe," p. 252.

35. Bankston, "A Literary Crown," scrapbook clipping.

36. Jones, "The Girl in the Universe," pp. 324-35.

37. *Ibid.*, p. 382.

38. *Ibid.*, p. 383.

39. Bankston, "A Literary Crown," scrapbook clipping.

40. Letter to James K. Murphy from C.M. Carthew-Yorstoun, Dallas, Texas, May 7, 1973.

41. Jones, "The Girl in the Universe," pp. 409-10.

42. *Ibid.*, p. 412.

43. *Ibid.*, p. 382.

44. Foster, "Editorial: Will N. Harben," scrapbook clipping.

45. Wallace Putnam Reed, "The Struggles of a Georgia Novelist," Atlanta *Journal*, n.d., scrapbook clipping.

46. Will N. Harben to Joel Chandler Harris, April 23, 1900, letter in the Harris Collection, Robert W. Woodruff Library, Emory University.

47. Reed, "The Struggles of a Georgia Novelist," scrapbook clipping.

48. "Innocents Abroad," Dalton *Citizen-News*, n.d., scrapbook clipping.

49. Johnson, "Will N. Harben," p. 8; a Dalton inhabitant who was told this story by Loveman gave Miss Johnson the information.

50. Will N. Harben, "American Backgrounds for Fiction: Georgia," *Bookman*, 38 (October, 1913), 188.

Chapter Two

1. "White Marie," Toledo *Journal*, n.d., scrapbook clipping.

2. "Personal Gossip About Writers," *Author*, 2 (June, 1890), 91-92.

3. "White Marie," New Orleans *States*, April 20, 1890, p. 4.

4. "With the Magazinists," Atlanta *Constitution*, November 24, 1889, p. 3.

5. Jones, "Life and the Girl," p. 165.

6. *White Marie: A Story of Georgia Plantation Life* (New York: 1889), pp. 27, 3.

7. "With the Magazinists," p. 3.

8. "White Marie," New York *Journal*, December 8, 1889, p. 9.

9. *White Marie*, pp. 44-45.

10. *Ibid.*, p. 134.

11. "White Marie," *Sunday Gazetteer*, n.d., scrapbook clipping.

12. Will N. Harben, "Mr. Harben's Rejoinder," Atlanta *Constitution*, December 15, 1889, p. 4.

13. Robert Bush, "Will N. Harben's Northern Georgia Fiction," *Mississippi Quarterly*, 20 (Spring, 1967), 105.

14. H. A. Wrench, "Another Version of 'White Marie'," Atlanta *Constitution*, December 8, 1889, p. 2.

15. Harben, "Mr. Harben's Rejoinder," p. 4.

16. H. A. Wrench, " 'White Marie' Again," Atlanta *Constitution*, December 22, 1889, p. 2.

17. "A Sermon on Literature," Knoxville *Tribune*, December 1, 1889, p. 2.

18. Will N. Harben, "A Critic Answered," Knoxville *Tribune*, December 8, 1889, p. 6.

19. M. C. Williams, "Books Reviewed by M. C. Williams," *Epoch*, 6 (January 17, 1890), 808.

20. Mrs. Lee C. Harby, "Correspondence," *Epoch*, 6 (January 31, 1890), 838.

21. M. C. Williams, "Correspondence," *Epoch*, 7 (February 7, 1890), 854.

22. Jones, "Life and the Girl," p. 168.

23. Charles H. George, "Sights of Gay New York: Author of 'White Marie'," Baltimore *American*, January 5, 1890, p. 5.

24. "Personal Gossip About Writers," n.p.: n.d., scrapbook clipping.

25. Jones, "The Girl in the Universe," p. 409.

26. *Almost Persuaded* (New York: 1890), pp. 161, 109, 101.

27. *Ibid.*, pp. 311-12.

28. "Almost Persuaded," New York *Commercial Advertizer*, March 13, 1891, p. 3.

29. B. O. Flower, "Almost Persuaded," *Arena*, 3 (April, 1891), xxxiv.

30. Tom Horan, "Dalton Writer Leaves His Name in Literary History," Dalton *Citizen-News*, March 27, 1970, p. 10.

31. Walter Leon Sawyer, "Prominent Authors: Will N. Harben," Boston *Weekly Journalist*, n.d., scrapbook clipping.

32. *A Mute Confessor* (Boston: 1892), p. 94.

33. "A Mute Confessor," Minneapolis *Tribune*, n.d., scrapbook clipping.

34. Sawyer, "Prominent Authors," scrapbook clipping.

35. *Ibid.*

36. Neith Boyce, "Books of the Day," *Arena*, 7 (February, 1893), xi.

37. *A Mute Confessor*, p. 93.

38. Hesekiah Butterworth to Editor, *Century Magazine*, n.d., letter in the Century Collection, New York Public Library.

39. Wallace Putnam Reed, "The Struggles of a Georgia Novelist," scrapbook clipping.

40. Jones, "Life and the Girl," p. 168.

41. "Will Harben a Consular Possibility," Atlanta *Constitution*, July 22, 1893, p. 3.

42. "The Passing Throng," Atlanta *Constitution*, n.d., scrapbook clipping.

43. Vernon Louis Parrington, Jr., *American Dreams: A Study of American Utopias* (Providence, Rhode Island: 1947), pp. 148-49.

44. *The Land of the Changing Sun* (New York: 1894), p. 105.

45. *Ibid.*, p. 66.

46. Parrington, *American Dreams*, p. 149.

47. Quoted in Walter Bogle, "75 Years Ago: Will Harben, Dalton Writer, Gains Salutes," Dalton *Citizen*, April 29, 1971, p. 2.

48. Claude R. Flory, *Economic Criticism in American Fiction 1792 to 1900* (New York: Russell and Russell, 1969), p. 237.

49. Kenneth M. Roemer, "1984 in 1894: Harben's *Land of the Changing Sun*," *Mississippi Quarterly*, 26 (Winter, 1972-73), 42.

50. "Will N. Harben's Syndicate Letters," leaflet distributed by Harben to Southern newspapers, scrapbook clipping.

51. Frank L. Stanton, "Just from Georgia," Atlanta *Constitution,* n.d., scrapbook clipping.

52. "Good One on Stanton," n.p.: n.d., scrapbook clipping.

53. Stanton, "Just from Georgia," scrapbook clipping.

54. "Will N. Harben Wedded," Dalton *Citizen-News,* July 3, 1896, p. 3.

55. *Ibid.*

56. Johnson, "Will N. Harben," pp. 11-12; the quotation appears in a letter from Harben's sister to Miss Johnson.

57. Maybelle Chandler Harben Mears, "Memoirs," first unpublished essay by Harben's wife, in possession of William N. Harben, Arlington, Virginia, p. 4.

58. *Ibid.*

59. For a discussion of the conventional elements of detective fiction, see Vincent Buranelli, *Edgar Allan Poe* (New Haven, Connecticut: College and University Press, 1961), pp. 80-86.

60. "From Clue to Climax," *Lippincott's,* 57 (June, 1896), 770, 777.

61. *The Caruthers Affair* (London and New York: 1898), pp. 202, 124.

62. One other detective novel, *The North Walk Mystery,* appeared in 1899. It is the only novel by Harben that I could not locate, despite exhaustive searches. Even though the National Union Catalog cites copies in the Library of Congress and at the University of Georgia, both copies have been lost.

Chapter Three

1. "Mr. Harben's Georgia Sketches," New York *Times Saturday Review of Books and Art,* December 8, 1900, p. 902.

2. Bush, "Will N. Harben's Northern Georgia Fiction," p. 105.

3. Will N. Harben to A. N. Johnson, April 4, 1895, letter in the Century Collection, New York Public Library.

4. "At Mrs. Frank Leslie's," *New England Homestead,* n.d., scrapbook clipping.

5. "The Tragic Story of Sunset Rock, Tennessee," *Current Literature,* 1 (August, 1888), 190.

6. "Aunt Nelly's Visit," *Youth's Companion,* 63 (December 4, 1890), 658.

7. "They Come and Go," n.p., September 19, 1895, scrapbook clipping.

8. Will N. Harben to Richard Watson Gilder, August 25, 1902, letter in the Century Collection, New York Public Library.

9. "Two Wanderers," *Dixie,* 7 (December, 1890), 999.

10. "The Frog-Boy," *Chaperone*, 2 (January, 1891), 426.

11. The other categories in which prizes were awarded were Descriptive, Queer, Dramatic, and Humorous.

12. "Her Children: An Etching," *Short Stories*, 9 (January, 1892), 60.

13. "Jim Knew: An Etching," *Short Stories*, 4 (January, 1891), 141.

14. "Not a Child Born," *Twentieth Century*, 6 (January 1, 1891), 13.

15. "A Cohutta Valley Shooting Match," *Outing*, 14 (November, 1891), 108.

16. "The Matrimonial Troubles of Abraham and Caroline," *Round Table*, 1 (May 3, 1890), 10-12.

17. "In the Year Ten Thousand," *Arena*, 6 (November, 1892), 744.

18. "Matt Digby's Meddling," *Lippincott's*, 56 (July, 1895), 114.

19. "A Touch of Nature," *Outlook*, 54 (November 21, 1896), 911.

20. "The Burial Arrangements of Elder Womack," *Woman's Home Companion*, 24 (March, 1897), 4.

21. "The Shortest Road to a Man's Heart," *Woman's Home Companion*, 24 (September, 1897), 1, 20, 2.

22. "The Return of the Inconstant," *Woman's Home Companion*, 25 (October, 1898), 7, 8.

23. "A Mountain Match-Maker," *Century*, 64 (July, 1902), 418.

24. "A Filial Pretence," *Harper's Monthly*, 107 (July, 1903), 260.

25. "Over the Mountain," *Era*, 12 (October, 1903), 347.

26. "Two Birds with One Stone," *Century*, 70 (May, 1905), 70.

27. "A Sprightly Heroine," *Harper's Weekly*, 49 (December 16, 1905), 13.

28. "The Sale of the Mammoth Western," *Century*, 75 (November, 1907), 82.

29. Bush, "Will N. Harben's Northern Georgia Fiction," p. 105.

30. Promotional leaflet distributed by A. C. McClurg & Co., in the Anthony Collection, New York Public Library.

31. Will N. Harben to Joel Chandler Harris, April 23, 1900, letter in the Harris Collection, Robert W. Woodruff Library, Emory University.

32. *Northern Georgia Sketches* (Chicago: 1900), p. 5. All further references to the stories in this collection will be supplied in parentheses in the text. See "Selected Bibliography," pp. [156-59] below, for information about their original magazine publication.

33. "Mr. Harben's Georgia Sketches," p. 902.

34. Bush, "Will N. Harben's Northern Georgia Fiction," p. 107.

35. *Ibid.*

36. *Ibid.*

37. McClurg promotional leaflet.

38. Will N. Harben to Richard Watson Gilder, April 5, 1901, letter in the Century Collection, New York Public Library.

Chapter Four

1. Mears, "Memoirs," p. 7.
2. *Ibid.*
3. *Ibid.*, p. 5.
4. *Ibid.*, p. 6.
5. *Ibid.*
6. *Ibid.*, p. 5.
7. *Ibid.*
8. *Ibid.*, p. 6.
9. *Ibid.*, p. 7.
10. Maybelle Chandler Harben Mears, "Looking Back," second unpublished essay by Harben's wife, in possession of Mrs. Judy Harben Alger, Clifton Park, New York, p. 3.
11. If this poem is an indication of the quality of Loveman's poetry, Harben's own poetic taste must be questioned, since he had earlier praised Loveman's merit as a poet. In all fairness to Loveman, though, the poem was a friendly gesture on his part, and not intended for publication.
12. Mark Pace, "His Aunt Was Mrs. Will Harben," Dalton *Citizen-News,* March 1, 1963, p. 4.
13. Will N. Harben to William G. Brown, October 17, 1911, letter in the William Garrott Brown Collection, Duke University Library.
14. Johnson, "Will N. Harben," pp. 27-28; the material is quoted from a letter to Miss Johnson from Mrs. Mears.
15. *Ibid.*, p. 27.
16. Will N. Harben to Marcelle Stanton, November 7, 1904, letter in the Stanton Papers, Robert W. Woodruff Library, Emory University.
17. Moses, "Why Will N. Harben Found in That Country and Its People Interesting Material for His Story-Building," p. 3.
18. *Ibid.*
19. *The Woman Who Trusted* (Philadelphia: 1901), p. 229. Further references to the novel are provided in parentheses in the text.
20. "News from New York," Philadelphia *Times,* January 10, 1890, p. 4.
21. *Westerfelt* (New York and London: 1901), p. iii. Further references to the novel are provided in parentheses in the text.
22. Harper & Row contract files, New York.
23. William Dean Howells, "Editor's Easy Chair," *Harper's Monthly,* 103 (October, 1901), 826.
24. William Dean Howells, "Mr. Harben's Georgia Fiction," *North American Review,* 191 (March, 1910), 359.
25. Carl Hovey, "Mr. Harben's 'Abner Daniel'," *Bookman,* 16 (September, 1902), 55.

26. "Abner Daniel," New York *Times Saturday Review of Books and Art,* July 5, 1902, p. 452.

27. Hovey, "Mr. Harben's 'Abner Daniel'," p. 55.

28. *Abner Daniel* (New York and London: 1902), p. 312. Further references to the novel are provided in parentheses in the text.

29. Harben, "American Backgrounds," p. 191.

30. *Ibid.,* p. 190.

31. *Ibid.,* p. 191.

32. William H. Honan, "Le Mot Juste for the Moon," *Esquire,* 72 (July, 1969), 56, 139.

33. *Ibid.,* p. 56.

34. "A Tale of Atonement," New York *Times Saturday Review of Books and Art,* April 25, 1903, p. 280.

35. *The Substitute* (New York and London: 1903), p. 195. Further references to the novel are provided in parentheses in the text.

36. Howells, "Mr. Harben's Georgia Fiction," p. 361.

37. Memo from Harben to Harper and Brothers, November 28, 1903, Harper & Row contract files, New York.

38. *The Georgians* (New York and London: 1904), p. 3. Further references to the novel are provided in parentheses in the text.

39. Will N. Harben to Richard Watson Gilder, September 30, 1904, letter in the Century Collection, New York Public Library.

40. "Another Southern Novel," *Independent,* 57 (October 6, 1904), 798-99.

41. James MacArthur, "Books and Bookmen," *Harper's Weekly,* 48 (November 5, 1904), 1701.

42. *Pole Baker* (New York and London: 1905), p. 48. Further references to the novel are provided in parentheses in the text.

43. Bush, "Will N. Harben's Northern Georgia Fiction," p. 110.

44. "Books and Bookmen," *Harper's Weekly,* 67 (March 7, 1903), 394.

45. *Ibid.*

46. Bush, "Will N. Harben's Northern Georgia Fiction," p. 110.

47. "Harben's Heart Was in Dixie," p. 6.

48. Harben, "American Backgrounds," p. 189.

49. *Ibid.*

50. *Ann Boyd* (New York and London: 1906), p. 14. Further references to the novel are provided in parentheses in the text.

51. Howells, "Mr. Harben's Georgia Fiction," p. 362.

52. "The Tender Link," *Ladies' Home Journal,* 15 (September, 1898), 3-4; Luke King had used "Lucian Laramore" as his pen name in the short story.

53. Harper & Row contract files, New York.

54. Mears, "Looking Back," p. 5.

55. "Mr. Will N. Harben's New Story of Rustic Life in Northern Georgia," New York *Times Saturday Review of Books,* October 13, 1906, p. 669.

56. "Ann Boyd," *Literary Digest,* 33 (October 13, 1906), 513-14.

57. Bush, "Will N. Harben's Northern Georgia Fiction," p. 111.

58. "Ann Boyd," *Independent,* 62 (January 24, 1907), 211.

59. Will N. Harben to Joel Chandler Harris, November 11, 1906, letter in the Harris Collection, Robert W. Woodruff Library, Emory University.

60. *Mam' Linda* (New York and London: 1907), p. 102. Further references to the novel are provided in parentheses in the text.

61. Harper & Row contract files, New York.

62. Mears, "Memoirs," pp. 5, 6; Jones, "The Girl in the Universe," pp. 273-74.

63. Jones, p. 274.

64. *Gilbert Neal* (New York and London: 1908), p. 3. Further references to the novel are provided in parentheses in the text.

65. Bush, "Will N. Harben's Northern Georgia Fiction," pp. 111-12.

66. "Gilbert Neal," *Nation,* 87 (November 5, 1908), 442-43.

67. "One Man's Redemption," New York *Times Saturday Review of Books,* October 9, 1909, p. 591.

68. "The Redemption of Kenneth Galt," *Nation,* 89 (October 28, 1909), 407.

69. Howells, "Mr. Harben's Georgia Fiction," p. 358.

70. *Ibid.*

71. *Dixie Hart* (New York and London: 1910), p. vii. Further references to the novel are provided in parentheses in the text.

72. Harben, "American Backgrounds," p. 190.

73. Harper & Row contract files, New York.

Chapter Five

1. Letter to James K. Murphy from Elizabeth Harben Cox, Darien, Connecticut, April 19, 1973.

2. Will N. Harben to George Duneka, July 15, 1910, letter in the Harper & Row contract files, New York.

3. *The Fruit of Desire* (New York and London: 1910), p. 294. Further references to the novel are provided in parentheses in the text.

4. "A Tolstoyan Tale," New York *Times Saturday Review of Books,* August 6, 1910, p. 436.

5. "Out of the Dark," New York *Times Review of Books,* August 20, 1911, p. 508.

6. *Nobody's* (New York and London: 1911), p. 97. Further references to the novel are provided in parentheses in the text.

7. *Jane Dawson* (New York and London: 1911), p. 24. Further references to the novel are provided in parentheses in the text.

8. *Paul Rundel* (New York and London: 1912), p. 63.

9. "A Story of the South," New York *Times Review of Books,* September 28, 1913, p. 495.

10. "The Desired Woman," *Nation,* 97 (November 6, 1913), 436.

11. *The Desired Woman* (New York and London: 1913), pp. 366-67. Further references to the novel are provided in parentheses in the text.

12. *The New Clarion* (New York and London: 1914), p. 2. Further references to the novel are provided in parentheses in the text.

13. *The Inner Law* (New York and London: 1915), p. 132.

14. "The Inner Law," New York *Times Review of Books,* October 3, 1915, p. 356.

15. "Second Choice," New York *Times Review of Books,* December 3, 1916, p. 536.

16. "Some of the Latest Autumn Fiction," *Literary Digest,* 53 (November 18, 1916), 1338.

17. *Second Choice* (New York and London: 1916), p. 319. Further references to the novel are provided in parentheses in the text.

18. "The Triumph," New York *Times Review of Books,* September 2, 1917, p. 326.

19. "Among the 'Localists'," *Nation,* 95 (September 20, 1917), 316-17.

20. Bush, "Will N. Harben's Northern Georgia Fiction," p. 114.

21. *The Triumph* (New York and London: 1917), p. 297. Further references to the novel are provided in parentheses in the text.

22. Harben, "American Backgrounds," p. 186.

23. Bush, "Will N. Harben's Northern Georgia Fiction," pp. 113-14.

24. Joyce Kilmer, "The Novel Must Go: Will N. Harben," *Literature in the Making by Some of Its Makers* (New York: 1917), pp. 187-91.

25. Johnson, "Will N. Harben," p. 20.

26. Letter to James K. Murphy from C. M. Carthew-Yorstoun, Dallas, Texas, May 7, 1973.

27. Mears, "Memoirs," p. 5.

28. Kilmer, "The Novel Must Go," p. 191.

29. Mears, "Looking Back," pp. 3-5.

30. Johnson, "Will N. Harben," p. 16. Miss Johnson credits this statement to a newspaper article by Kenneth Groesbeck eulogizing Harben, sent to her by Harben's widow. The title and source of the article are unknown.

31. Mears, "Looking Back," p. 5.

32. Letter to James K. Murphy from George Harben, New York, New York, August 10, 1973.

33. *Ibid.*

34. Mears, "Looking Back," pp. 1-2.
35. Letter to James K. Murphy from Elizabeth Harben Cox, Darien, Connecticut, September 23, 1973.
36. "Will N. Harben Dead," New York *Times,* August 8, 1919, p. 9. Harben's widow later married an editor from Harper and Brothers, and she and her husband died within half an hour of each other in 1945. She was buried beside Harben in Dalton.
37. *The Cottage of Delight* (New York and London: 1919), p. 427.
38. Johnson, "Will N. Harben," p. 20.
39. Bush, "Will N. Harben's Northern Georgia Fiction," p. 115.
40. Will N. Harben to Robert Sterling Gordon, December 24, 1915, letter in the Anthony Collection, New York Public Library.
41. *The Divine Event* (New York and London: 1920), pp. 96, 51.

Chapter Six

1. William Dean Howells, *My Mark Twain: Reminiscences and Criticisms* (New York and London: Harper and Brothers, 1910), p. 49.
2. William Dean Howells to Samuel L. Clemens, February 11, 1910, in *Life in Letters of William Dean Howells,* ed. Mildred Howells (Garden City, New York: Doubleday and Company, Inc., 1928), II, 281.
3. Jones, "The Girl in the Universe," p. 3.
4. Kilmer, "The Novel Must Go," pp. 195-96.
5. Howells, "Mr. Harben's Georgia Fiction," p. 360.
6. Harben, "American Backgrounds," pp. 186-87.
7. Howells, "Mr. Harben's Georgia Fiction," pp. 357-58.
8. Harben, "American Backgrounds," p. 188.
9. Howells, "Mr. Harben's Georgia Fiction," p. 359.
10. Kilmer, "The Novel Must Go," pp. 192-93.
11. Bush, "Will N. Harben's Northern Georgia Fiction," p. 110.
12. Harben, "American Backgrounds," p. 188.
13. Moses, "Why Will N. Harben Found in That Country and Its People Interesting Material for His Story-Building," p. 3.
14. Harben, "American Backgrounds," p. 187.
15. Moses, "Why Will N. Harben . . . ," p. 3.
16. Howells, "Mr. Harben's Georgia Fiction," p. 360.
17. Moses, "Why Will N. Harben . . . ," p. 3.
18. Howells, "Mr. Harben's Georgia Fiction," p. 363.

Selected Bibliography

PRIMARY SOURCES

1. Books

Abner Daniel. New York and London: Harper and Brothers, 1902.
Almost Persuaded. New York: Minerva Publishing Company, 1890.
Ann Boyd. New York and London: Harper and Brothers, 1906.
The Caruthers Affair. London and New York: F. Tennyson Neely, 1898.
The Cottage of Delight. New York and London: Harper and Brothers, 1919.
The Desired Woman. New York and London: Harper and Brothers, 1913.
The Divine Event. New York and London: Harper and Brothers, 1920.
Dixie Hart. New York and London: Harper and Brothers, 1910.
The Fruit of Desire. New York and London: Harper and Brothers, 1910. (Published under the name "Virginia Demarest.")
The Georgians: A Novel. New York and London: Harper and Brothers, 1904.
Gilbert Neal: A Novel. New York and London: Harper and Brothers, 1908.
The Hills of Refuge. New York and London: Harper and Brothers, 1918.
The Inner Law. New York and London: Harper and Brothers, 1915.
Jane Dawson: A Novel. New York and London: Harper and Brothers, 1911.
The Land of the Changing Sun. New York: The Merriam Company, 1894; Boston: Gregg Press, 1975; New York: AMS Press, 1975.
Mam' Linda. New York and London: Harper and Brothers, 1907.
A Mute Confessor: The Romance of a Southern Town. Boston: Arena Publishing Company, 1892.
The New Clarion: A Novel. New York and London: Harper and Brothers, 1914.
Nobody's. New York and London: Harper and Brothers, 1911. (Published under the name "Virginia Demarest.")
The North Walk Mystery. New York: Street and Smith, 1899.
Northern Georgia Sketches. Chicago: A. C. McClurg and Company, 1900; Freeport, New York: Books for Libraries Press, 1970.

156

Paul Rundel: A Novel. New York and London: Harper and Brothers, 1912.
Pole Baker: A Novel. New York and London: Harper and Brothers, 1905.
The Redemption of Kenneth Galt. New York and London: Harper and Brothers, 1909.
Second Choice: A Romance. New York and London: Harper and Brothers, 1916.
The Substitute. New York and London: Harper and Brothers, 1903.
The Triumph: A Novel. New York and London: Harper and Brothers, 1917.
Westerfelt: A Novel. New York and London: Harper and Brothers, 1901.
White Marie: A Story of Georgia Plantation Life. New York: Cassell and Company, 1889.
The Woman Who Trusted: A Story of Literary Life in New York. Philadelphia: H. Altemus Company, 1901.

2. Magazine Articles and Stories
"American Backgrounds for Fiction: Georgia," *Bookman,* 38 (October, 1913), 186-92.
"Aunt Dilsey's Son," *Youth's Companion,* 65 (June 16, 1892), 306-07.
"Aunt Milly's Surprise," *Youth's Companion,* 63 (October 16, 1890), 530-31.
"Aunt Nelly's Visit," *Youth's Companion,* 63 (December 4, 1890), 658-59.
"Before Two Altars," *Ladies' Home Journal,* 10 (May, 1893), 3-4; (June, 1893), 7-8.
"Br'er Cato's Power," *Chaperone,* 4 (December, 1891), 255-62.
"The Burial Arrangements of Elder Womack," *Woman's Home Companion,* 24 (March, 1897), 3-4; (April, 1897), 7-8, 19.
"Circus Dan," *Delineator,* 75 (March, 1910), 210-11.
"A Cohutta Valley Shooting Match," *Outing,* 14 (November, 1891), 107-12.
"The Convict's Return," *Lippincott's,* 63 (April, 1899), 549-62.
"The Courage of Ericson," original source unknown; published in newspapers of the Bacheller Syndicate, and included in *Northern Georgia Sketches.*
"A Dog's Role,"*Independent,* 42 (January 9, 1890), 26-27.
"The Duel at Frog Hollow," *Short Stories: A Magazine of Select Fiction,* 10 (August, 1892), 439-50.
"The Elixir," *Independent,* 46 (Feburary 1, 1894), 26-27.
"A Fair Exchange," *Lippincott's,* 69 (January, 1902), 115-24.
"A Filial Impulse," *Century,* 59 (January, 1900), 363-71.

"A Filial Pretence," *Harper's Monthly*, 107 (July, 1903), 252-60.
"Fred's Mother," *Youth's Companion*, 65 (April 7, 1892), 170-71.
"The Frog-Boy," *Chaperone*, 2 (January, 1891), 420-26.
"From Clue to Climax," *Lippincott's*, 57 (June, 1896), 737-816.
"Gid Sebastian's Probation," *Independent*, 43 (June 4, 1891), 38-39.
"He Came and Went Again," *Arena*, 4 (September, 1891), 494-502.
"Her Children: An Etching," *Short Stories: A Magazine of Select Fiction*, 9 (January, 1892), 60.
"The Heresy of Abner Calihan," *Ladies' Home Journal*, 11 (July, 1894), 7-8.
"A Humble Abolitionist," *Black Cat*, 5 (January, 1900), 28-44.
"In the Year Ten Thousand," *Arena*, 6 (November, 1892), 743-49.
"Jacob Ladd's Change of Heart," *Youth's Companion*, 64 (October 1, 1891), 517-18.
"Jim Knew: An Etching," *Short Stories: A Magazine of Select Fiction*, 4 (January, 1891), 141.
"Jim Trundle's Crisis," *Lippincott's*, 61 (March, 1898), 412-21.
"John Bartow," *Youth's Companion*, 62 (September 5, 1889), 433-34.
"The Maltby's Son," *Independent*, 43 (January 1, 1891), 30-31.
"Martha," *Youth's Companion*, 62 (December 26, 1889), 685-86.
"The Matrimonial Troubles of Abraham and Caroline," *Round Table*, 1 (May 3, 1890), 10-12; reprinted as "Abrum, Ca'line and Asphalt," *Short Stories: A Magazine of Select Fiction*, 5 (March, 1891), 148-58.
"Matt Digby's Meddling," *Lippincott's*, 56 (July, 1895), 108-14.
"A Message from the Stream," *Youth's Companion*, 62 (October 24, 1889), 518-19.
"A Million-Dollar Cinder," original source unknown; copy in Harben's scrapbook, belonging to Mrs. Elizabeth Harben Cox, Darien, Connecticut.
"A Mother's Verdict," *Independent*, 43 (October 8, 1891), 26-28.
"A Mountain Match-Maker," *Century*, 64 (July, 1902), 413-22.
"Not a Child Born," *Twentieth Century*, 6 (January 1, 1891), 12-13.
"On the Road to Marlet," *Woman's Home Companion*, 24 (October, 1897), 3-4.
"Over the Mountain," *Era*, 12 (October, 1903), 341–48.
"A Prophet Without Honor," original source unknown; copy in Harben's scrapbook, belonging to Mrs. Elizabeth Harben Cox, Darien, Connecticut.
"A Question of Valor," *Century*, 66 (July, 1903), 442–53.
"The Return of the Inconstant," *Woman's Home Companion*, 25 (October, 1898), 7-8.
"Ring Joe," *Independent*, 42 (April 24, 1890), 30-31; reprinted as "The Story of Ring Joe," *Short Stories: A Magazine of Select Fiction*, 3 (November, 1890), 139-48.

"A Rural Visitor," *Book News*, 16 (May, 1898), 523-29.
"The Sale of the Mammoth Western," *Century*, 75 (November, 1907), 74-84.
"The Sale of Uncle Rastus," *Lippincott's*, 54 (September, 1894), 403-09.
"The Shortest Road to a Man's Heart," *Woman's Home Companion*, 24 (September, 1897), 1-2, 20-21.
"A Sprightly Heroine," *Harper's Weekly*, 49 (December 16, 1905), 10-13.
"The Tender Link," *Ladies' Home Journal*, 15 (September, 1898), 3-4.
"Thicker Than Water," *Book News*, 16 (November, 1893), 99-110.
"A Tie of Blood," *Woman's Home Companion*, 25 (May, 1898), 5-6.
"A Touch of Nature" [essay], *Outlook*, 54 (November 21, 1896), 911-12.
"A Touch of Nature" [short story], *Youth's Companion*, 65 (December 8, 1892), 645-46.
"The Tragic Story of Sunset Rock, Tennessee," *Current Literature*, 1 (August, 1888), 188-90.
"Two Birds with One Stone," *Century*, 70 (May, 1905), 61-70.
"Two Points of View," *Independent*, 48 (December 3, 1896), 34-35.
"Two Wanderers," *Dixie*, 7 (December, 1890), 996-99.
"The Whipping of Uncle Henry," *Lippincott's*, 58 (December, 1896), 828-38.
"White Jane," *Youth's Companion*, 62 (July 11, 1889), 350-51.

3. Manuscript Collections Containing Letters of Will N. Harben
Anthony Collection, Manuscripts and Archives Division, New York Public Library, Astor, Lenox and Tilden Foundations.
William Garrott Brown Papers, Duke University Library.
Century Collection, Manuscripts and Archives Division, New York Public Library, Astor, Lenox and Tilden Foundations.
Joel Chandler Harris Collection, Special Collections Department, Robert W. Woodruff Library, Emory University.
Personal scrapbooks of Harben's short stories and newspaper clippings pertaining to him, belonging to Mrs. Elizabeth Harben Cox, Darien, Connecticut.
Frank L. Stanton Papers, Special Collections Department, Robert W. Woodruff Library, Emory University.

SECONDARY SOURCES

"Books and Bookmen," *Harper's Weekly*, 67 (March 7, 1903), 394. Appreciative article offering reasons for Harben's popularity to date.
BUSH, ROBERT. "Will N. Harben (1858-1919)." Louis D. Rubin, Jr., ed.,

A Bibliographical Guide to the Study of Southern Literature. Baton Rouge: Louisiana State University Press, 1969. Short bibliography of works to date about Harben.

———. "Will N. Harben's Northern Georgia Fiction," *Mississippi Quarterly,* 20 (Spring, 1967), 103-17. The most perceptive and complete critical essay on Harben. Includes solid discussions of several of the novels.

"Harben, Will(iam) N(athaniel)," *Who's Who in America, 1918-1919,* X, 1182. Standard biographical information.

"Harben, William Nathaniel," *Authors Digest,* XIX, 243. Short biographical sketch, accompanied by condensation of *Abner Daniel* by Harben himself in Volume Nine.

"Harben, William Nathaniel (Will N.)," *The National Cyclopaedia of American Biography,* X, 310-11. Additional biographical information, more complete than most.

"Harben's Heart Was in Dixie," Richmond *Evening Journal,* August 19, 1919, p. 6. Sincere, accurate, elegaic article.

HART, BERTHA SHEPPARD. *Introduction to Georgia Writers.* Macon, Georgia: J. W. Burke Company, 1929. Emphasis on Harben's style, characters, and 1913 essay for *Bookman,* "American Backgrounds for Fiction: Georgia."

HONAN, WILLIAM H. "Le Mot Juste for the Moon," *Esquire,* 72 (July, 1969), 53-56, 139. Amusing article incidentally crediting Harben with rural terms used by modern astronauts.

HORAN, TOM. "Dalton Writer Leaves His Name in Literary History," Dalton *Citizen-News,* March 27, 1970, p. 10. Reflections of Harben by a friend and fellow Daltonian.

HOWELLS, WILLIAM DEAN. "Mr. Harben's Georgia Fiction," *North American Review,* 191 (March, 1910), 356-63. The first important critical analysis of Harben's works. Appreciative overall, but honest in perceiving Harben's flaws.

JOHNSON, ROSE B. "Will N. Harben, Georgia Novelist." M.A. Thesis, University of Georgia, 1925. Interesting for Miss Johnson's correspondence with Harben's family and friends, offering information not found elsewhere.

JONES, KATHERINE HARBEN. "Life and the Girl" and "The Girl in the Universe." Unpublished memoirs of Harben's youngest sister, belonging to Mrs. Aileen F. Alley, Dalton, Georgia. Haphazardly written, but valuable for insights into early life of Harben and his family.

KILMER, JOYCE, ed. *Literature in the Making by Some of Its Makers.* New York: Harper and Brothers, 1917. Includes interesting interview with Harben, who expresses ideas about the writing of novels and about the current state of novels in general.

McKINNEY, ANNIE BOOTH. "Will N. Harben." Edwin Anderson Alderman and Joel Chandler Harris, eds., *Library of Southern Literature*, Vol. V. Atlanta: Martin and Hoyt Company, 1907, pp. 2073-97. Solid analysis of Harben's writing to date, followed by excerpt from *Abner Daniel* and complete short story, "The Sale of the Mammoth Western."

MEARS, MAYBELLE CHANDLER HARBEN. "Looking Back" and "Memoirs." Unpublished essays by Harben's wife, in possession of Mrs. Judy Harben Alger, Clifton Park, New York, and William N. Harben, Arlington, Virginia. These short reflections of life with a famous writer by Harben's widow offer insights into Harben's life in New York City.

MOORE, VIOLET. "Dalton Writer Will Harben Depicts State Mountain Life," Macon *Telegraph*, July 11, 1973, p. 3A. A modern Georgian discovers the quaintness of life in Harben's works.

MOSES, VIVIAN M. "Why Will N. Harben Found in That Country and Its People Interesting Material for His Story-Building," New York *Times*, August 13, 1905, Sec. 3, p. 3. Useful discussion of Harben's method, chiefly in Harben's own words.

MURPHY, JAMES K. "The Backwoods Characters of Will N. Harben," *Southern Folklore Quarterly*, 39 (September, 1975), 291-96. Review of some of Harben's mountain characters.

———. "Georgia's Journalistic Jesters," *Georgia Life*, 2 (Autumn, 1975), 18-19. Light account of the newspaper bantering between Frank L. Stanton and Harben.

———. "Will N. Harben's 'Virginia Demarest' Novels: An Addendum," *Mississippi Quarterly*, 29 (Winter, 1975-76), 105-08. Short article on Harben's two novels written under a pseudonym.

PARRINGTON, VERNON LOUIS, JR. *American Dreams: A Study of American Utopias*. Providence, Rhode Island: Brown University, 1947. Contains several pages devoted to Harben's utopian novel, *The Land of the Changing Sun*.

ROEMER, KENNETH M. "1984 in 1894: Harben's *Land of the Changing Sun*," *Mississippi Quarterly*, 26 (Winter, 1972-73), 28-42. Sees Harben's science-fiction novel as prophetic of the tradition of the later Huxley-Orwell works.

RUTHERFORD, MILDRED LEWIS. *The South in History and Literature*. Atlanta: Franklin-Turner Company, 1907. Brief, rather overdone sketch.

VAN DOREN, CARL. *Contemporary American Novelists, 1900-1920*. New York: Macmillan Company, 1922. Although merely mentioning Harben as practitioner of local color, first chapter offers a delightfully perceptive analysis of the movement.

WADE, JOHN D. "Harben, William Nathaniel," *Dictionary of American Biography*, VIII, 238. One of the best short discussions of Harben and his works.

Index

A. C. McClurg & Co., 69
Arena, 39, 57, 59
Atlanta *Constitution*, 26, 34, 47

Book News, 57, 60
Bookman, 126
Boone, Daniel, 15, 16, 25
Boston *Courier*, 46
Bryan, Mary E., 82
Burnett, Frances Hodgson, 49; *See also*
　Little Lord Fauntleroy
Bush, Robert, 103, 124

Cable, George Washington, 52
Cassel and Company, 29
Century Magazine, 42-43, 57, 66, 71,
　96, 111
Chandler, Joe, 48
Chandler, Maybelle (wife), 48-49,
　78-80, 82, 131, 155n36
Chaperone, 60
Chattanooga *Times*, 53
Clemens, Samuel L., 53, 78-79, 112,
　127, 136-37, 144; *See also*
　Huckleberry Finn
Cooper, James Fenimore, 18, 143-44
Cooper, Leroy Gordon, 91
Cort Theater, 106
Cosby, William, 15
Current Literature, 53

Dallas *Morning News*, 25; *See also*
　Dealy, George
Dalton, Georgia, 15-25, 27, 28, 34, 36,
　43, 48, 49, 57, 62, 90, 98, 99, 111,
　131, 139, 155n36
"Darley," 15, 83, 87, 90, 92, 94, 97, 99,
　103, 104, 107, 117, 120
Davis, Richard Beale, 71
Davis, Richard Harding, 41

Dealy, George, 25; *See also* Dallas
　Morning News
Delineator, 68
"Demarest, Virginia," 113-15, 128
Dixie, 58
Doyle, Arthur Conan, 29, 44, 49-50
Dreiser, Theodore, 78, 85, 144
DuMaurier, George, 44, 139

Edward VII, 79
Eliot, T. S., 116, 144
Emerson, Ralph Waldo, 116, 144
Epoch, 35
Esquire, 91

Faller, James, 106; *See also Hotheads,*
　The
Flory, Claude R., 46
Flower, B. O., 39

Garland, Hamlin, 41, 78
Gilder, Richard Watson, 57, 110
Glasgow, Ellen, 78
Goddard, Robert, 91
Grady, Henry W., 26, 27

Haggard, H. Rider, 44
Harben, Georgia Monterey, 17, 19
Harben, Katherine, 17, 19, 20, 23-24,
　25, 26, 30, 35, 36, 48, 107, 137,
　146n34
Harben, Matilda Frances, 17, 19, 48
Harben, Nathaniel Parks (father), 15,
　16, 18, 19, 20-21, 24, 69, 87, 107,
　121, 127
Harben, Tommie, 16, 17
Harben Tyre R., 18
Harben, Walter LaFayette, 17, 19-22,
　23, 24, 25, 123
Harben, Will N.: ancestry, 15-16,

162

4425

PS
1788
H3
Z78

Murphy, James K.

Will N. Harben

DATE			